THE LORIMER POCKETGUIDE TO

ONTARIO
BIRDS

Written and illustrated by Jeffrey C. Domm

James Lorimer & Company Ltd., Publishers
Toronto

James Lorimer & Company Ltd. acknowledges the support of the Government of Canada through the Book Publishing Industry Development Program (BPIDP) for our publishing activities.

Canadian Cataloguing in Publication Data

Domm, Jeffrey C., 1958-
        Lorimer pocketguide to Ontario birds / written & illustrated by Jeffrey C. Domm.

Includes index.
ISBN-13: 978-1-55028-920-6
ISBN-10: 1-55028-920-9

        1. Birds--Ontario--Identification. 2. Bird watching--Ontario--Guidebooks.
I. Title.

QL685.5.O5D665 2006   598'.09713   C2006-900752-7

Cartography by Peggy McCalla

James Lorimer & Company Ltd., Publishers
317 Adelaide Street West
Suite #1002
Toronto, ON M5V 1P9
www.lorimer.ca

Printed and bound in China

Contents

Contents

Introduction

Southern Ontario is an excellent place to enjoy birdwatching. A rich mosaic of forest, meadow, river, lake, marsh, and beach, it is home to a wide variety of breeding birds and year-round residents, and on the migration path for dozens of other species on their seasonal journeys between breeding and wintering grounds. In summer and fall, hundreds of species can be identified around the province, many of them in full mating plumage.

It can be difficult to identify wild birds correctly, especially if they are a great distance away and foliage or other obstacles are blocking your view. The full-colour illustrations in this book, along with the visual keys and the descriptions, will help you quickly compare essential features.

Each illustration has been drawn especially for this guide from photographs, live observation, scientific specimens and written descriptions. They represent typical specimens. When comparing a bird with the illustration, one has to bear in mind that plumage varies from individual to individual. Many birds change plumage seasonally and the colours change in different light conditions.

This book is divided into two sections: Water Birds and Land Birds. Within each section, the birds are arranged into groups such as gulls, raptors or warblers, and birds that are of similar type and size are in close proximity.

Of the hundreds of birds that either reside in or pass through southern Ontario, a selection of 225 familiar species was chosen for this book. In addition to the very common and widespread birds, there are those that have limited habitat but are of great interest to birdwatching enthusiasts. Birds that breed in Ontario are identified by an accurate illustration of their egg. The list of Birding Hot Spots (pages 12-26), selected by Ted Cheskey, Co-ordinator of the Important Bird Area Program for Ontario Nature, will guide you to accessible areas across southern Ontario that experienced birdwatchers have found to be excellent birding sites.

Before setting out on a birdwatching trip, be sure to dress warmly and watch the weather. High winds or a sudden drop in temperature can affect the number of birds you see, as well as dampen your spirits if you are not well prepared. Experienced birders also recommend you leave your valuables at home and lock your car doors before you leave it to go birding.

With the help of this guide you will find that birdwatching is both rewarding and full of surprises. As you begin to recognize many of the birds of eastern North America, you will appreciate their abundant variety.

How to Use This Guide

Birds don't stay in one place for very long, so it is important to learn a few simple rules to help you quickly identify them. You will often see waterfowl or shorebirds either feeding or flying. If a bird is on the water, you can watch to see if it dives, skims the surface or tips its head under water, leaving its tail feathers pointing to the sky. If it is flying, you can observe the beating pattern of its wings — are they quick wingbeats, is it soaring, does it flap its wings and then glide?

Viewing land birds is a bit different. Most often what you see is a bird that is feeding; perhaps it is hopping along the ground or flitting from branch to branch. Maybe it is perched in a tree, preparing to fly away.

The visual keys given in this guide focus on the primary identifiable features of each bird, and include colour, outline and size. Because water birds are more often seen in flight than land birds, and have a wider variety of food-gathering methods, we have also included flying pattern and feeding style.

Secondary features for both kinds of birds include foot type, egg colour and size, and observation calendar.

When you are looking at a bird, first estimate the size, then take note of the shape of the wings, tail, head, bill or beak and feet. Note any particular marks — patches, streaks, stripes and speckles. Finally, observe its movements.

Legend for visual keys

1 **Size identification** — the rectangle represents the page of this book, and the silhouette of the bird represents its size against this page.

2 **Foot type** — Tridactyl

Anisodactyl   Zygodactyl

3 **Flight characteristics** —

Quick wingbeats

Slow steady wingbeats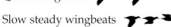

Soaring

Wingbeats followed by gliding

Category of Bird

1

Size Identification

2

Foot Type

3

Flying

4 **Feeding technique** —

Stabs and prodding motion

Grazing and dabbling

Diving head first

Dives from water's surface

Tip up feeding

Skims water surface

Feeding

5 **Egg** — actual size and shape unless otherwise indicated.

Egg

6 **Backyard feeder** — there are three types of bird feeders to which small birds might be attracted.

7 **Birdhouse nester** — some species are happy to make their nest in a manmade house, which you might hang in your garden.

Backyard Feeder

8 **Nesting location** (for inland birds only)

▼ Hollow in ground

▼ Waterside plants

▼ Bushes and thickets

▼ Cavities of trees

▼ Deciduous trees

▼ Conifers and tall trees

▼ Tall, dead, decaying trees

▼ Banks along rivers and ponds

▼ Cliffs and/or rocky ledges

Birdhouse Nester

Nesting Location

9 **Observation calendar** — the bar gives the initial for each of the twelve months of the year. The deeper colour indicates the best months for seeing the species, according to known migration patterns.

Observation Calendar

Quick Reference Index

Step 1: Determine the approximate size of bird in relation to page size.

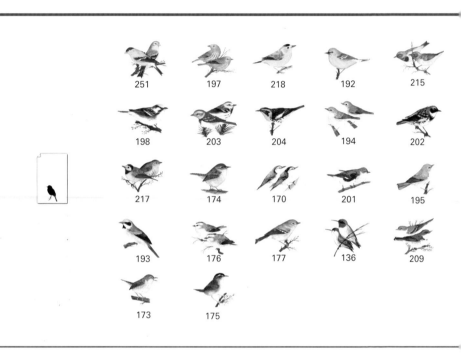

251	197	218	192	215
198	203	204	194	202
217	174	170	201	195
193	176	177	136	209
173	175			

216	151	224	220	229
228	182	166	214	225
213	183	155	141	84
221	234	163	233	207

252   100   91   83   92

191   161   116   179   68

242   102   189   244

93   154   188   75   82

86   124   90   108   88

184   243   236   77   74

94   133   54   99   43

62   80   117   118   49

48   79   44   51   160

95   96   97   64   128

127   129   71   31   61

45   46   98   57   125

58   115   28   121   39

152 78 180 132 73 87

148 245 237 81 185 240

186 72 137 122 123 126

187 153 241 158 76 139

162 143 142 67 140 89

138 56 101 41 42 55

38 47 144 37 36 29

59 50 52 70 69 159 53

107 110 111 34 35 112

120 105 33 66 40 119

109 131 114 130 63 32

65 106 113 30 60 104

Birding Hot Spots

"Hot spots" are the sites experienced birders identify as the best places to observe birds in the wild. Below are 100 of Southern Ontario's hottest birding spots, selected by Ted Cheskey, Co-ordinator of the Important Bird Area program for Ontario Nature. "Important Bird Areas ", sites recognized as important for the conservation of bird populations, are marked with a star. Please consult a current provincial road map for directions or contact hot spot sites directly for information on access and entry fees.

Southwestern Ontario

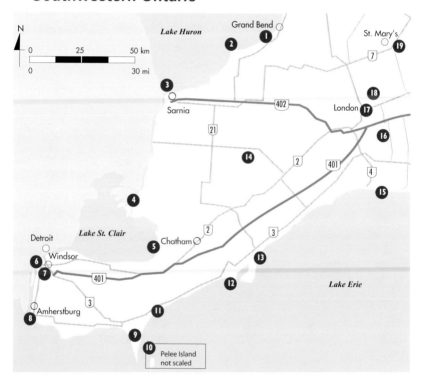

1 Pinery Provincial Park – Port Franks*

Best birding is along the Ausable River channel, at the Visitor's Centre feeders, and in the campgrounds. Specialties include Eastern Towhee, Whip-poor-will, and American Woodcock. In March Tundra Swans congregate near Greenway Road.

2 Kettle Point*

This is an excellent location in the fall to observe migrating loons and waterfowl. During migration watch for Red-bellied and Red-headed Woodpeckers along the network of forested cottage roads.

3 **Point Edward***

The lighthouse marks the outlet of Lake Huron, where waterfowl, gulls and the occasional jaeger species are funnelled after a strong cold front in the fall. Don't forget to check for land birds!

4 **Walpole Island***

This huge delta prairie and wetland has amazing birds. Egrets, herons, ducks, rails and coots are seen in wetlands and fields. Best to hire a guide for access to the most interesting locations.

5 **St. Clair National Wildlife Area and Eastern Lake St. Clair***

A system of dykes and viewing towers allows access to marshes rich in wetland birds. Rails, herons, egrets, waterfowl, and Bald Eagles can be observed in the spring, summer or fall. Black-bellied Plovers stop in fields between Bradley and Mitchell's Bay in early to mid May and Tundra Swans can be seen in March.

6 **Windsor – Detroit River***

In the fall and winter and early spring, large numbers of waterfowl, including Canvasback and Redhead, congregate along the Detroit River, easily observed from parkland.

7 **Windsor – Ojibwa Prairie**

In southwest Windsor, the Ojibwa prairie provides a mix of woodlands and prairie where southern species such as Carolina Wren, Northern Cardinal and many migrants can be observed.

8 **Holiday Beach Conservation Area***

Best known in the fall for migrating hawks that pass over the park, some days in the thousands, this hot spot is spectacular all seasons. Wetlands, woodlands, shoreline and a viewing platform make for great birding.

9 **Point Pelee National Park***

One of the best birding sites in North America, Pelee's birding peaks in May when trees can drip with warblers, tanagers, vireos and grosbeaks, and the ground can move with thrushes and sparrows. Watch for Red-breasted Merganser on the lake and check the tip for gulls and shorebirds.

10 **Pelee Island***

A mixture of open woods, farms, vineyards and nature reserves, Pelee Island offers great opportunities for birding. Watch for Yellow-breasted Chat, cuckoos and migrants in the spring.

⑪ Wheatley Provincial Park

Birding within the park is excellent in May when many species of warblers and flycatchers, Scarlet Tanagers, Rose-breasted Grosbeaks, Indigo Buntings and many other species stop in the vegetation. A trip to Hillman Marsh will add a great number of water birds!

⑫ Erieau*

The harbour hums with gulls and terns in the spring and fall. Check for Forster's and Common Terns and Bonaparte's Gulls. The McGeachy Pond Conservation Area nearby is rich in water birds and shorebirds.

⑬ Rondeau Provincial Park*

The endangered Prothonotary Warbler nests in the lowland swamp forests. A good trail system through forest and coastal wetlands makes birding in the spring extremely productive. Rondeau Bay is one of the best waterfowl viewing locations on the Great Lakes.

⑭ Skunk's Misery*

Near Newbury are hundreds of hectares of public and private forest with breeding Wood Thrush, Red-eyed Vireo, pewees, grosbeaks, redstarts and rare species such as Hooded Warbler. Be prepared for mosquitoes in the spring.

⑮ Hawk Cliff*

At Hawk Cliff, the fall migration of raptors peaks during the second or third week of September. Sharp-shinned and Cooper's Hawks pass at tree-top, while high overhead, you might see a "kettle" of Broad-winged Hawks.

⑯ Aylmer Wildlife Management Area*

This is one of the best locations in Ontario to observe Tundra Swans in March and early April. An observation tower facilitates viewing of Bufflehead, Ring-necked Duck and other waterfowl.

⑰ Westminster Ponds/Pond Mills Conservation Area

This large area is one of the best locations near London to observe migrants. It also has resident Great Horned Owls, Eastern Wood-Pewees, Baltimore Orioles, Red-eyed Vireos, and other widespread species.

⑱ Fanshawe Park Conservation Area

This conservation area has a large reservoir used by waterfowl in the spring and fall. Many land birds including, warblers, Gray Catbird and sparrows, can be found along the Riverside Trail.

19 **Wildwood Lake Conservation Area**

Visible from Highway 7 near St. Marys, this large reservoir attracts ducks such as Mallard, American Black Duck, Ring-necked Duck, Lesser Scaup, Bufflehead and mergansers. Large numbers of gulls roost on the reservoir.

South-central Ontario – Georgian Bay – Lake Huron

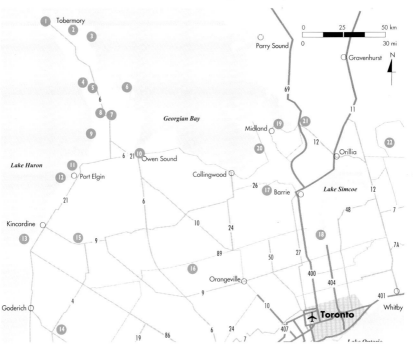

1 **Tobermory**

Headlands and bays around Tobermory are migrant traps in spring and fall; sparrows, warblers and other land birds can be abundant in April and May. Migrating hawks, waterfowl, loons and grebes can be seen from shoreline observation points.

2 **Bruce National Park**

The Cypress Lake Campground provides great year-round birding. In spring and summer watch and listen for Black-throated Green Warbler, American Redstart, White-throated Sparrow, Hermit and Swainson's Thrush and Whip-poor-will.

3 Dyer's Bay and Cabot Head*

The pastures and woodlands near Dyer's Bay are rich in open-country species such as meadowlarks, kingbirds and bluebirds. Sandhill Cranes and American Bitterns frequent wet fields and wetlands. Check Georgian Bay for grebes, loons and mergansers, and the Cabot Head lighthouse for migrants. Bruce Peninsula Bird Observatory operates a migration monitoring station nearby.

4 Stokes Bay

Black Creek Provincial Park has rich mixed forests with many warbler species such as Blackburnian and Black-and-white. In the winter look for northern finches such as Pine Siskin and White-winged Crossbill.

5 Ferndale Flats

Flat, open farmland south of Ferndale is home to Red-winged Blackbirds, Savannah Sparrows and Wilson's Snipe in wet areas. In the winter, check for Rough-legged Hawk and Snowy Owl.

6 6. Cape Croker Indian Park and Campground

On First Nations land, the open prairie along Sidney Bay has breeding Savannah and Grasshopper Sparrows. The forests around the campground have breeding Wood Thrush, Rose-breasted Grosbeak and pewees.

7 Wiarton

Colpoy's Bay is worth checking for waterfowl. At Purple Valley, Least Flycatchers, Yellow-bellied Sapsuckers and hummingbirds nest in the forests and hawks migrate along the escarpment in the spring.

8 The Rankin River and Isaac Lake

Isaac Lake, accessible off Highway 6 and Bruce Road 13, harbours breeding Black Terns, Osprey, Wood Ducks and Belted Kingfishers. Black-crowned Night Heron, rails and bitterns are seen or heard in the wetlands off Isaac Lake Road.

9 Oliphant and Red Bay

Shorebirds such as Wilson's Snipe, Yellowlegs, Least Sandpiper and Semipalmated Plover use the coastal mudflats, seen from shoreline roads. Offshore are the Fishing Islands, nesting grounds for Common Terns, Caspian Terns, Ring-billed and Herring Gulls.

10 Owen Sound

Inglis Falls, Hibou and Ainslie Woods Conservation Areas include mature mixed forest with typical woodland birds, among them nuthatches, phoebes, Black-and-white Warblers and Hairy and Pileated Woodpeckers. The bay itself is used by waterfowl, loons and grebes.

11 **Southampton – Miramichi Bay**

Offshore lies Chantry Island, a migratory bird sanctuary with nesting cormorants, herons, Great Egrets, gulls, terns and Bald Eagles. Miramichi Bay is one of the best shorebird sites along Lake Huron. Watch for Ruddy Turnstones and all types of waders.

12 **MacGregor Point Provincial Park**

Home to the Huron Fringe birding festival, there is great birding in the campground where Veery, American Redstart and Black-throated Green Warblers are common. The wetlands at the south end have gnatcatchers, Blue-winged Warblers, Least Bitterns, Soras and Wood Ducks.

13 **Point Clark**

Point Clark projects into Lake Huron, allowing viewing opportunities in the fall for migrating waterfowl, loons, gulls and species that otherwise avoid land, known by birders as "pelagics."

14 **Hullet Provincial Wildlife Management Area**

This large system of dyked wetlands and associated forest provides fine spring opportunities, with few other visitors, to observe waterfowl, harriers, rails, bitterns and even land birds.

15 **Grenoch Swamp Wetland Complex**

This large forested wetland between Walkerton and Kincardine is a good location to observe Wood Duck and many land birds such as Veery, Common Yellowthroat and Northern Waterthrush.

16 **Luther Marsh Wildlife Management Area**

This vast wetland complex has many species of nesting waterfowl, bitterns, herons, egrets, Northern Harrier, American Woodcock and Wilson's Snipe. The surrounding habitats attract northern species to breed, such as Nashville Warbler and Lincoln's Sparrow.

17 **Minesing Swamp**

This wetland is accessible by road or, even better, canoe. Gnatcatchers, Veery, Wood Duck, Wilson's Snipe, Marsh Wren and bitterns are among the more than 100 species you could encounter here.

18 **Holland Marsh Provincial Wildlife Area**

The Holland Marsh includes extensive wetland habitat where Yellow Warbler, Common Yellowthroat, Savannah Sparrow, Northern Harrier and Wilson's Snipe can be found. There is board-walked access to the wetlands.

19 Wye Marsh Provincial Wildlife Area*

Along with the visitor's centre, the interpretive trails give information about the wetlands and forests they access. Wetlands have breeding Black Tern, bitterns, Pied-billed Grebe, rails, Common Moorhen and American Coot. The site is best known for rearing Trumpeter Swans for reintroduction into the wild; these swans have now established themselves across much of Ontario.

20 Tiny Marsh Provincial Wildlife Area *

Several wetland compounds with varying amounts of vegetation attract water birds, including Pied-billed Grebe, ducks, geese, herons, rails and Black Tern. The viewing is good along dykes and from an observation tower.

21 21. Matchedash Bay Provincial Wildlife Area*

This bay contains extensive wetlands, with the full complement of wetland species including, Least Bitterns. Adjacent forest is rich in land birds such as vireos, Golden-winged Warblers and American Redstarts.

22 Carden Plain*

The cattle ranches and limestone plains provide savannah-like landscape teeming with breeding meadowlarks, Upland Sandpipers, Brown Thrashers, Vesper Sparrows, Golden-winged Warblers, kingbirds, and many other species.

The Golden Horseshoe

1 South Walsingham – Backus Woods — St. Williams Forestry Station*

This is one of the largest forest complexes in southern Ontario, and home to numerous warblers, flycatchers, the Scarlet Tanager, thrushes and raptors. Many rare species, such as Hooded Warbler, are common in places.

2 Port Rowan

Visit the Bird Studies Canada (BSC) Headquarters' wetland and trail overlooking Long Point Bay for shorebirds, waterfowl, land birds and raptors such as Bald Eagle. Check out what BSC is doing to monitor and protect birds in Canada and abroad.

3 Long Point*

The Long Point Peninsula stretches 30 km due east, forming a large bay to the north. The causeway and

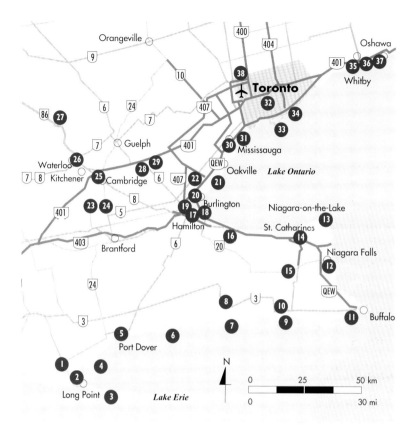

marshes include parts of a National Wildlife Area. The road east leads to Long Point Provincial Park. The entire area is spectacular for land birds and water birds alike. Watch for Purple Martins and Red-headed Woodpeckers in the Park and Bald Eagles and Northern Harrier over the marshes.

4 Turkey Point*
This park is rich old-oak savannah forest, with land birds such as Wood Thrush, Eastern Towhee, Eastern Bluebird, Great Crested Flycatcher and Rose-

breasted Grosbeak being common. Listen at night for Whip-poor-wills.

5 Port Dover
The Port Dover harbour has good food and good birding. Terns, gulls, loons, grebes and ducks are seen in the harbour. Watch for agile Bonaparte's Gulls in spring and fall.

6 Selkirk Provincial Park
This park boasts a bird banding station, oak woodland and shoreline that attracts land birds and water birds. Southerners such as Carolina

Wren mingle with northern migrants in the spring and fall. Northern Saw-whet Owls overwinter in the park.

7 Rock Point Provincial Park
Spring and fall, this is one of the best locations along Lake Erie to see shorebirds. Check the shoreline for Yellowlegs, Sanderlings, Ruddy Turnstones, Pectoral Sandpipers, Semipalmated Sandpipers, Black-bellied Plovers and more.

8 Dunnville
Marshes extend from Dunnville almost to the mouth of the Grand River. Herons, egrets, bitterns, rails, coots, Common Moorhens, Marsh Wrens, terns and swallows can be observed spring, summer and fall.

9 Port Colborne*
A large mixed colony of gulls and terns nest on the breakwalls. The Common Tern colony persists (from being taken over by Ring-billed Gulls), thanks to a professor and his students from Brock University and local stewards from Port Colborne.

10 Wainfleet Bog
Despite drainage and peat extraction, this expansive wetland is a fine birding location where Northern Harriers, Whip-poor-wills, Wilson's Snipes, and a mix of other northern and southern species breed.

11 Fort Erie*
Waterfowl congregate in the mouth of the Niagara River in the late fall and winter. Watch the daily movements of gulls and ducks, among them Canvasbacks, Redheads, Common Goldeneyes and Buffleheads.

12 Niagara Falls*
Plan a visit in the fall and behold thousands of gulls. Some birders observe a dozen species in a day, Bonaparte's Gull being perhaps the most numerous. Check the river for diving ducks and loons.

13 Niagara-on-the-Lake
The Niagara River (the entire river is designated an Important Birding Area) empties into Lake Ontario at Niagara-on-the-Lake. Fall birding is good, with movements of gulls along the shoreline (especially late in the day), and land birds such as Carolina Wren and Northern Mockingbird as possibilities.

14 St. Catharines
Port Weller, the entry to the Welland Canal, has a 2-km-long weir with woods and openings that are attractive for migrants. There are also good opportunities to see waterfowl and water birds.

15 Upper 12 Mile Creek*
The rich woodlands and ravines of Short Hills Provincial Park and St. Johns

Conservation Area, between St. Catharines and Fonthill, harbour many forest-breeding birds, including Scarlet Tanager, Wood Thrush and Hooded Warbler.

16 Beamer Conservation Area*
Located on Grimsby Mountain, Beamer is best known for the spring migration of vultures, hawks, falcons and eagles. Visit in April and marvel at the passage of hawks overhead and the counters who keep track of them.

17 Tollgate Ponds/ Windermere Basin*
"Build and they will come" is the story behind the colonies of gulls, terns and cormorants that nest on these artificial peninsulas. Watch for Black-crowned Night Herons, also at the colony.

18 Van Wagner's Beach
Visit in the fall, when an easterly blows, park near Hutch's restaurant and observe the spectacle of huge rolling waves, and the parade of ducks, geese, gulls and even jaegers blown in from the lake.

19 Royal Botanical Gardens Nature Centre and Cootes Paradise*
Hamilton is an exceptional place to bird year-round, and the RBG Nature Centre and extensive property, including Cootes Paradise, is a must-visit area. The Nature Centre trails allow access to the north part of Cootes Paradise and a wide range of woodland birds including pewees, Northern Cardinals and friendly Black-Capped Chickadees. The trails and tower on the south side of Cootes Paradise offer great viewing of wetland species of all types.

20 Woodland Cemetery
Located on a high bluff over Hamilton Harbour, this cemetery is a migrant trap. The mature trees attract woodland birds, and the panorama of Hamilton Bay provides good views of migrating raptors.

21 Paletta/McNichol/ Shoreacres Park
Situated between Walker's and Appleby lines are good views of Lake Ontario. From October to April watch for Bufflehead, Goldeneye, other waterfowl, and wrens, woodpeckers and migrants during migration.

22 Bronte Provincial Park
Within the heart of Burlington, Bronte Provincial Park is an oasis for land birds during migration. Trails allow access to the heavily forested ravine, where Indigo Bunting, Gray Catbird and Rose-breasted Grosbeak breed.

23 Bannister-Wrigley Lake Conservation Area

This forest and wetland complex has accessible trails and good birding. Very friendly Black-capped Chickadees live in nearby Dickson Wilderness Area. Sandhill Cranes, Trumpeter Swans, American Coots, Pied-billed Grebes and many ducks frequent Bannister Lake in the fall.

24 Cambridge to Paris Rail Trail

Running parallel to the Grand River, this trail traverses deep forest, edge, and meadowland, habitat for Baltimore Oriole, Chestnut-sided Warbler, and Warbling Vireo. Bald Eagle, Common Merganser and Common Goldeneye use the open river in the winter.

25 Forks of the Grand and Speed rivers, Cambridge

Accessed from the Riverbank Trail or the Walter Bean Trail, this area includes riverside, mature forest, and a mixture of edge habitats that are well used by migrants. Bald Eagles regularly overwinter.

26 Laurel Creek Conservation Area

This park is excellent for waterfowl and gulls from fall to early winter and early to mid spring. Least Bittern, Sora and Virginia Rail nest in the marsh.

27 Floradale Reservoir and raptor fields

The sparsely forested farmland is a reliable spot to observe Rough-legged Hawk, and possibly Snowy Owl in wintertime. Snow Buntings and Horned Larks are seen along roads or in fields. Check north end of reservoir for Shorebirds in late and early fall.

28 Valens Conservation Area

An observation tower and boardwalk provide opportunities to observe Wood Ducks, Pied-billed Grebes and Marsh Wrens. White-throated Sparrow and Veery breed in the mixed forest near the campground.

29 Mountsberg Conservation Area

This large reservoir and wetland has excellent spring, summer and fall birding. Ospreys, Pied-billed Grebes, Green Herons and numerous other water birds are observed here. Turkey Vultures are never far away. The Birds of Prey Centre is worth a visit.

30 Rattray's Marsh

Located near downtown Mississauga, this hot spot includes an extensive woodland and marsh with a viewing platform where ducks, water birds and shorebirds can be observed.

31 Colonel Samuel Smith Park

This migrant trap, near the mouth of the Humber River, has ponds, marshes and a viewing platform. Watch for Horned Larks and Snow Buntings in the winter and for ducks on the lake.

32 High Park

This huge urban park, undergoing restoration to oak savannah, is a magnet for migrating land birds. The marsh at the north end of Grenadier Pond is used by rails and several duck species.

33 Toronto Islands

The Island Nature Sanctuary just north of the Island Nature School is good for migrant land birds. All of the beaches and remaining woodlots can be good birding spots during migration.

34 Tommy Thompson Park*

This landfill known as the "Spit" has good birding year-round. Most significant is a huge multi-species bird colony of Ring-billed Gull, Double-crested Cormorant and Black-crowned Night Heron. In the bay, watch for Long-tailed Duck in the winter.

35 Cranberry Marsh and Lynde Shores

Cranberry Marsh is an expansive wetland with boardwalks and viewing towers. A hawk migration watch takes place in September and October. Nearby Lynde Shores woodlot has a friendly flock of Black-capped Chickadees and is worthwhile checking year-round.

36 Thickson Woods

This small but productive forest in Oshawa is a must visit during the spring migration, when land birds concentrate. Great Horned Owls often nest in this forest.

37 Second Marsh

North of the marsh is extensive woodland with good trails and a viewing tower. East is another viewing tower and a trail to Lake Ontario. Rails, herons, waterfowl and Marsh Wrens use the marsh, and in late spring and fall many shorebirds visit the extensive mudflats along the western side.

38 Clairville Conservation Area

This park has much diversity in a small area. In the winter, the conifer plantations are used by owls, including Northern Saw-whet and Long-eared owls, as roosting sites.

Southeastern and Eastern Ontario

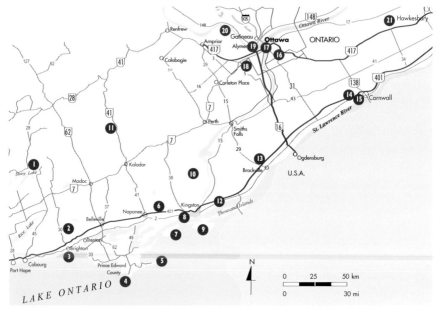

1 Petroglyph Provincial Park
Look for woodpeckers, White-winged Crossbill and Evening Grosbeak in the park's bogs and pine forests, among other northerly species. Watch for Bald and Golden Eagles scavenging deer carcasses in winter months.

2 Murray Marsh Conservation Area
South of Percy Reach on the Trent River is this large swamp wetland. Breeding rails, bitterns and Wood Ducks are present in marshy areas and Northern Waterthrush, Common Yellowthroat and Veery can be spotted in the forest.

3 Presqu'ile Provincial Park*
Perhaps the best all-round birding location in Ontario, Presqu'ile's combination of deep forest, open forest, meadow, marsh, mudflats, beach and rocky shoals attracts all types of birds. Shorebirds such as Short-billed Dowitchers, Sanderlings and Dunlin are best viewed in May and from August to October. A huge colony of cormorants, gulls and herons breed on Gull and High Bluff islands. Waterfowl of all types appear in the Bay or on the lake. Land-bird viewing during breeding season, and especially in spring migration, can be spectacular.

4 Point Petre Provincial Wildlife Area*
This site offers very good remote birding during

migration. Watch for White-winged Scoter, Long-tailed Duck, Bufflehead, mergansers and other ducks on the lake.

5 Prince Edward Point National Wildlife Area*

A superb location with forest, meadows and a banding station, PEP is both a migrant trap, excellent for spotting migrating land birds, and a place with superb views of Lake Ontario for observing migrating loons, grebes and ducks.

6 Napanee Barrens*

Explore the roads north and east of Napanee where the barren landscape attracts uncommon scrubland-breeding species such as cuckoos, thrashers, towhees, bluebirds and the very rare Loggerhead Shrike.

7 Amherst Island*

Bundle up and explore Amherst Island in the winter, when birds of prey concentrate here. Watch for Short-eared Owls, Snowy Owls and Snow Buntings in fields, and Northern Saw-whet Owls in the accessible cedar woodlots.

8 Kingston

Accessible Lemoine Point Conservation Area is a good place to see many water birds such as cormorants, Long-tailed Ducks, Scaups, Redheads, Canvasbacks, gulls and terns.

9 Wolfe Island

Wolfe Island is much like Amherst Island, with barren farmland, woodlots and, depending on the year and season, many owls and hawks feeding on cyclically abundant voles. Dress warmly in the winter!

10 Frontenac Provincial Park

This park provides opportunities to observe classic Canadian Shield species such as Common Loon, Great Blue Heron, Belted Kingfisher and Osprey, and a great variety of land birds from Yellow-bellied Sapsuckers to Ruffed Grouse.

11 Bon Echo Provincial Park

Bon Echo attracts northerly species such as Swainson's Thrush, Evening Grosbeaks and crossbills. Also watch for Pileated Woodpecker, Red-breasted Nuthatch, Broad-winged Hawk and a great variety of other land birds. Listen for Barred Owls at night.

12 Ivey Lea – Thousand Islands National Park

The St. Lawrence River at Ivy Lea is an excellent place to observe gulls, including the Greater Black-backed, and ducks, such as the Common Goldeneye, as well as Bald Eagles and other land birds.

13 Brockville

North of Brockville is Mac Johnson Conservation Area. A large forest, wetland and reservoir provide good birding opportunities.

14 Upper Canada National Migratory Bird Sanctuary

This Sanctuary east, of Morrisburg, has well-planned trails with viewing blinds that lead through a variety of habitats, from meadows to ponds. Geese, Mallards, American Black Duck, Northern Pintails and other waterfowl can be viewed, depending on the season.

15 Cornwall – Long Sault Parkway

The Long Sault Parkway offers good views of the St. Lawrence River. Watch for Great Black-backed, Iceland and Glaucous Gulls among the Herring and Ring-billed Gulls at the Saunders Dam and Power Station in winter.

16 Mer Bleu Conservation Area

East of Ottawa, Mer Bleu is a large forest with expansive peat bog. Many interesting northern species have nested here, including Lincoln's Sparrow and Sedge Wren, and Nashville, Yellow-rumped and even Palm Warblers.

17 Ottawa – Parliament Hill and the Parkway

From the base of Parliament Hill west along the Ottawa Parkway, shoreline vegetation and parkland attract migrants. In the winter waterfowl, including Common Goldeneye, can be seen on the churning river.

18 Sarsaparilla, Stoney Swamp and Jack Pine Trails

These conservation lands have good winter birding along the trails through mixed and coniferous forest. Watch for finches, chickadees, nuthatches and sparrows such as White-throated.

19 Brittania Conservation Area

Mud Lake, pine forest, deciduous woodland, and edge habitats in an urban setting combine to make a tremendous migrant trap. The Deschênes Rapids attracts many waterfowl, including Common Goldeneye in the winter.

20 Constance Bay

This bay in the Ottawa River, between Arnprior and Ottawa, is an excellent birding location year-round. Check for waterfowl, terns, shorebirds, land birds and hawks.

21 Alfred Bog

Southwest of Hawkesbury is the expansive Alfred Bog. Sandhill Cranes and Lincoln's Sparrows can be seen or heard along the boardwalk, and Short-eared Owls have nested in the bog.

Water Birds

With a wide variety of different habitats and many excellent birding sites, southern Ontario offers birders a wealth of opportunities to see waterfowl and shorebird species, both residents and migrants.

The southern Great Lakes shorelines are favourite feeding grounds for many gulls, shorebirds, waders and ducks. Shores, mudflats, and marshy areas associated with lakes, rivers, flooded fields, ponds, and even municipal sewage lagoons are home to many water birds. In the spring and fall, birders can enjoy one migration, one of the wonders of nature. Migrants, among them ducks, geese and many shorebirds, travel thousands of miles between their breeding grounds in the north and their winter homes in the south. Along the way, they stop to feed and to wait out inclement weather. These are perfect times to go birding.

The birds in this section are those that you are most likely to see in one of these habitats. Along with each full-colour illustration, there are visual keys depicting seasonal range, the size of the bird, the type of foot, its flight pattern and its characteristic way of feeding. The egg is shown for birds that breed in the province.

Common Loon
Gavia immer

Size Identification

Foot: Tridactyl

Flying

Feeding

Observation Calendar
J F M A M J J A S O N D

Male/Female: *Summer*: Black head and neck with white banded neck ring; thick grey sharp bill; red eye; white chest and belly; black back and wings spotted white; feet and legs black. *Winter*: Contrasting blacks and whites muted to dark dull brown. *In flight*: Large feet trail behind tail feathers; quick wing beats close to water's surface; takes off from water by running across surface.

Did you know? Loons can remain underwater for more than 5 minutes. They dive to feed and to avoid danger.

Voice: Drawn out *lou-lou-lou-lou* like yodelling, often at dusk or dawn.
Food: Small fish.
Nest/Eggs: Mound built with aquatic plants, mostly on islands. 2 eggs.

Egg: 75%

Pied-billed Grebe
Podilymbus podiceps

Foot: Tridactyl

Flying

Feeding

Observation Calendar
J F M A M J J A S O N D

Male/Female: *Summer*: Overall brown with grey-brown back; yellow eye ring; stout bill, white with distinct black band; black chin; short tail. *Winter*: White ring on bill softens; lighter chin. White tail feathers occasionally revealed when threatened by another bird. *In flight*: White patch on belly and white trail edge on wings.

Voice: Call is *cow* repeated with *keeech* at end, also various cluckings.
Food: Small fish, amphibians, crayfish, aquatic insects.
Nest/Eggs: Platform built with aquatic plants in shallow water attached to reeds and other aquatic plants. 5-7 eggs.

Egg: Actual Size

Horned Grebe

Podiceps auritus

Size Identification

Foot: Tridactyl

Flying

Observation Calendar

J F M A M J J A S O N D

Feeding

Male/Female: *Summer*: Dark wings and head; distinct golden ear tufts; reddish-brown neck and sides; white belly; feet and legs black; red eye. *Winter*: Dark grey upperparts; large white patch on cheek extending to back of head.

Did you know? The Horned Grebe tends to jump forward from the water's surface before diving to catch prey.

Voice: Usually quiet but occasionally makes loud croaks and chatters.
Food: Small fish, aquatic insects, crayfish, shrimp, insects, frogs, salamanders.

Snow Goose
Chen caerulescens

Size Identification

Foot: Tridactyl

Flying

Observation Calendar
J F M A M J J A S O N D

Male/Female: White overall with black primaries; short pink bill; feet and legs yellow; short tail.

Voice: High-pitched honk.
Food: Grains, seeds, grasses, aquatic plants, roots.

Feeding

Canada Goose

Branta canadensis

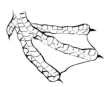

Observation Calendar

J F M A M J J A S O N D

Male/Female: Black head, neck and bill; white cheek patch; breast and belly pale brown with white flecks; feet and legs black; back and wings brown with white edging; short black tail; white rump, seen in flight. *In flight*: Flies in "V" formations.

Voice: Musical *honk*, repeated. Female slightly higher pitched *honk*.
Food: Grass, various seeds, sand, grain.
Nest/Eggs: Large nest of twigs, moss and grass, lined with down feathers, placed near water's edge. 4-8 eggs.

Mute Swan

Cygnus olor

Size Identification

Foot: Tridactyl

Flying

Observation Calendar

J F M A M J J A S O N D

Male/Female: White overall; bright orange or pink beak; black knob at base of beak; unique S-shaped neck when swimming; feet and legs black.

Did you know? The Mute Swan, native to Europe, was brought to North America in the nineteenth century as an ornamental species for parks and large estates.

Feeding

Voice: Mostly silent. Occasional hissing and barking or loud trumpet call.
Food: Fresh and saltwater plants, algae, grains.
Nest/Eggs: Large pile of grass and moss, lined with feathers, usually built on edge of pond or marsh. 4-6 eggs.

Egg: 55%

33

Size Identification

Trumpeter Swan
Cygnus buccinator

Foot: Tridactyl

Flying

Feeding

Observation Calendar

J F M A M J J A S O N D

Male/Female: Overall white; long neck; black bill; black skin extends from bill to eye; feet and legs black.

Voice: Bugle sounding *kah hah*.
Food: Aquatic plants, duckweed.
Nest/Eggs: Large platform built with twigs and other vegetation, near water. Often built on top of muskrat mounds or beaver dens. 4-6 eggs.

Egg: 60%

34

Tundra Swan

Cygnus columbianus

Size Identification

Foot: Tridactyl

Flying

Observation Calendar

J F M A M J J A S O N D

Male/Female: Overall white bird; black beak; yellow dash extending from eye down to base of beak, but not always present; black facial area narrowing to eyes; neck and head occasionally appear lightly rusted colour; feet and legs black.

Voice: High-pitched whistling. Bugling sound; *hoo-ho-hoo* when migrating.
Food: Aquatic plants, mollusks, grains.
Nest/Eggs: Platform built of aquatic plants, grasses and moss, on islands. 2-7 eggs.

Feeding

Wood Duck

Aix sponsa

Observation Calendar

J F M A M J J A S O N D

Male: Green head and drooping crest; black cheeks; red eye and white throat with two spurs; bill orange with black markings; chest brown with white spots leading to white belly; black and green back; sides tan with white and black band. *In flight*: Long squared tail.

Female: Back and crown brown; white eye ring; speckled breast and lighter coloured belly.

Voice: Male — high-pitched whistle. Female — loud *oooooeeek* in flight.

Food: Aquatic plants, insects, minnows, amphibians.

Nest/Eggs: In cavity of tree, as high as 20 metres, or in a log or built structure lined with wood chips and feathers. 9-12 eggs.

Gadwall

Anas strepera

Size Identification

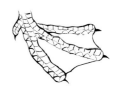

Foot: Tridactyl

Flying

Observation Calendar

J F M A M J J A S O N D

Male: Body overall grey-brown; black rump and tail feathers; light grey pointed feathers on back; feet and legs orange; thin black banding over entire body; black bill.
Female: Dull greyish brown and black overall; black bill with orange on sides.

Feeding

Voice: Male gives whistle and *rab rab* call. Quacking and high-pitched descending note from female.
Food: Seeds and aquatic plants.
Nest/Eggs: Nest built on islands from plant material and lined with down, slightly concealed. 7-13 eggs.

Egg: Actual Size

American Wigeon
Anas americana

Observation Calendar
J F M A M J J A S O N D

Male: White patch running up forehead from bill; green around eye broadening at cheeks and descending on neck; brown changing to black on back and extremely pointed wings; pointed tail feathers are black, with white lines; bill white with black patches on top and on tip. *In flight:* Green on trailing edge of wing; white forewing and belly.

Female: Overall light brown with brighter colour running down sides. No green patch on eye.

Did you know? The American Wigeon is an opportunist: waiting for other diving ducks to come to the surface with their catch, it will attempt to steal the food.

Voice: Male — occasional distinctive whistle *wh-wh-whew.* Female quacks.
Food: Aquatic plants.
Nest/Eggs: Grasses lined with down, concealed under brush or tree, a distance from water. 9-12 eggs.

American Black Duck

Anas rubripes

Size Identification

Foot: Tridactyl

Flying

Observation Calendar

J F M A M J J A S O N D

Male: Dark black with hint of brown overall and blue speculum; bill is olive; feet and legs orange. *In flight*: White patches under wings.
Female: Overall lighter brown than male with orange and black bill.

Voice: Both female and male *quack*. Male also whistles.
Food: Vegetation, insects, amphibians, snails, seed, grain, berries.
Nest/Eggs: Depression on ground, lined with grass, leaves and down, close to water's edge. 8-12 eggs.

Feeding

Egg: Actual Size

Mallard

Anas platyrhynchos

Size Identification

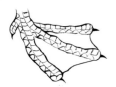

Foot: Tridactyl

Flying

Observation Calendar

J F M A M J J A S O N D

Feeding

Male: Bright green iridescent head, yellow bill; thin white collar; chestnut brown chest; grey sides; black and grey back; white tail; black curled feathers over rump; feet and legs orange. *In flight*: Blue speculum with white border, underparts of wings grey and brown.
Female: Overall brown streaked with orange bill, black patches on bill; white tail feathers.

Voice: Male — call soft *raeb* repeated. Female — loud *quacks* repeated.
Food: Aquatic plants, grain, insects.
Nest/Eggs: Shallow cup built of grasses and aquatic plants, lined with feathers on ground concealed near water. 8-10 eggs.

Egg: Actual Size

40

Blue-winged Teal

Anas discors

Foot: Tridactyl

Flying

Observation Calendar
J F M A M J J A S O N D

Male: Grey head with crescent-shaped white patch running up face, bill black; chest and belly brown; back and wings dark brown with buff highlights; blue and green speculum; feet and legs yellow.
Female: Overall brown speckled with pale blue speculum.

Voice: Male has high-pitched *peeeep*. Female — *quack* is soft and high-pitched.
Food: Aquatic plants, seeds.
Nest/Eggs: Pile of grasses lined with down, close to water's edge, concealed. 9-12 eggs.

Feeding

Egg: Actual Size

41

Northern Shoveler

Anas clypeata

Size Identification

Foot: Tridactyl

Flying

Observation Calendar

J F M A M J J A S O N D

Feeding

Male: Grey speckled head and neck; yellow eye; wide black bill; sides rust; mottled brown back. *In flight*: Green speculum; light blue wing patch.
Female: Overall brown with orange bill.

Voice: Low *quack* or *cluck*.
Food: Aquatic plants, duckweed, insects.
Nest/Eggs: Made from grasses in hollow on ground, lined with down feathers, at a distance from water. 8-12 eggs.

Egg: Actual Size

Northern Pintail

Anas acuta

Size Identification

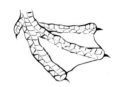

Foot: Tridactyl

Flying

Observation Calendar

J F M A M J J A S O N D

Feeding

Male: Brown head with white line circling around cheeks to chest; white chest and belly; back and wings are black and grey; long tail is black and brown; rump black; sides grey with thin black banding; bill grey with white line. *In flight*: Long tail; white neck and line running up neck.
Female: Overall brown with black bill; no pintail feature.

Voice: Male has two high-pitched whistles. Female quacks.
Food: Aquatic plants, seeds, crustaceans, corn, grains.
Nest/Eggs: Bowl of sticks, twigs, and grasses, lined with down, at a distance from water's edge. 6-9 eggs.

Egg: Actual Size

Green-winged Teal

Anas crecca

Observation Calendar
J F M A M J J A S O N D

Male: Head is rust with green patch running around eye to back of head; bill black; black at back of base of neck; warm grey body with thin black banding; distinctive white bar running down side just in front of wing; white rump; short square tail.
Female: Overall dull brown with green speculum; dark band running through eye.

Voice: Male — high pitched whistle. Female — weak shrill voice.
Food: Seeds, aquatic plants, corn, wheat, oats.
Nest/Eggs: On ground, cup shaped, filled with grasses and weeds, sometimes a distance from water. 10-12 eggs.

Canvasback

Aythya valisineria

Size Identification

Foot: Tridactyl

Flying

Observation Calendar

J F M A M J J A S O N D

Male: Dark reddish-brown head with sloping forehead; long black bill; black breast; grey wings; black tail; feet and legs black.
Female: Grey body; head and neck lighter brown.

Voice: Call is cooooing from male only. Female call is soft *krrr-krr* during courtship.
Food: Aquatic plants, roots, bulbs, insects, small fish, crustaceans.
Nest/Eggs: Bowl-like nest built from grasses and reeds then lined with feather down. Nest floats attached to aquatic plants. 7-12 eggs.

Feeding

Egg: Actual Size

45

Redhead

Aythya americana

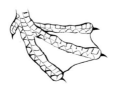

Observation Calendar

J F M A M J J A S O N D

Male: Deep red head; bluish bill with black tip; grey mottled overall; black breast.
Female: Brown body overall; dark brown back; white eye ring; darker crown.

Did you know? Females often lay their eggs in the nests of other ducks. Success is low because the host duck often deserts those eggs.

Voice: Male catlike during courtship.Female has soft growl.
Food: Aquatic vegetation, insects, larvae, molluscs, small crustaceans.
Nest/Eggs: Basket attached to aquatic plants such as cattails. 9-13 eggs.

Ring-necked Duck
Aythya collaris

Foot: Tridactyl

Flying

Observation Calendar

J F M A M J J A S O N D

Male: Back, head and breast black; high forehead; black bill with white outlines; yellow eyes; white spur on breast leading to grey underside and belly. *In flight*: Grey speculum; white belly.

Female: Grey cheeks and bill; one white band at tip of bill; white eye ring; dark charcoal back; brown chest, belly and sides.

Feeding

Voice: Male has low, loud whistle. Female call is soft *prrrrrrrr* notes. Mostly quiet.

Food: Aquatic plants, molluscs, insects.

Nest/Eggs: Cup-shaped, built of grasses and moss and lined with down feathers, concealed near pond. 8-12 eggs.

Egg: 90%

Greater Scaup

Aythya marila

Size Identification

Foot: Tridactyl

Flying

Feeding

Observation Calendar

J F M A M J J A S O N D

Male: *Winter*: Dark green iridescent head, neck and chest; white sides and belly; large flat grey bill; yellow eye; grey back with thin black banding; stubby black tail; black feet and legs. *Summer*: Sides and belly brown; head, neck and chest dull brown-black. *In flight*: Large white patches on inside of wings.

Female: Overall dark brown with white face patch. Head held lower than male. *In flight*: Large white patches on trailing edge of wings.

Voice: Male — repeated *waaahooo*. Female — growling *arrrrr*. Mostly quiet.

Food: Aquatic plants, crustaceans, molluscs, snails.

Lesser Scaup
Aythya affinis

Size Identification

Foot: Tridactyl

Flying

Observation Calendar

J F M A M J J A S O N D

Feeding

Male: Black head comes to peak at top toward back; head has purple tint in bright lighting; yellow eye; short narrow grey bill; dark breast and neck; grey-banded back; white sides and belly; dark rump and tail; feet and legs black.
Female: Dark brown overall with white patches on either side of bill. *In flight*: Long white banding down to tip on underside of wings.

Did you know? Large flocks, called "rafts," gather together by the thousands on the water in the winter.

Voice: Single note, low whistle, *wheeeooo*, and quacking.
Food: Aquatic seeds, crustaceans, insects, snails.

Surf Scoter
Melanitta perspicillata

Size Identification

Foot: Tridactyl

Flying

Feeding

Observation Calendar

J F M A M J J A S O N D

Male: Overall black with white patches on forehead and back of neck; yellow eye; distinctive large orange and red bill with black and white patches on sides.

Female: Overall dark brown with large black bill and vertical white patch behind it; top of head is slightly darker. *In flight:* Pale grey belly.

Did you know? Spotting the Surf Scoter is easy if you look for birds diving directly into the breaking surf hunting for molluscs or crustaceans.

Voice: Male — low whistle during courtship.
Food: Mussels, crustaceans, insects, aquatic plants.

White-winged Scoter

Melanitta fusca

Size Identification

Foot: Tridactyl

Flying

Observation Calendar

J F M A M J J A S O N D

Male: Black overall with yellow eye and white tear-shaped mark around eye; bill is orange, yellow and white; orange feet and legs. *In flight*: White wing patch.

Female: Brown overall; white oval on face; white patches on wings.

Voice: Male — in courtship is similar to ring of bell. Female — low whistle.

Food: Clams, scallops, mussels.

Feeding

Black Scoter

Melanitta nigra

Observation Calendar

J F M A M J J A S O N D

Male: Overall black with long thin tail feathers; large yellow knob on top of black bill; feet and legs dark orange.
Female: Overall dark grey with lighter grey on cheeks.

Voice: Low whistle during courtship. Quiet.
Food: Aquatic plants, molluscs, mussels, limpets.

Long-tailed Duck

Clangula hyemalis

Observation Calendar

J F M A M J J A S O N D

Male: *Winter*: White head with grey cheek and black patch; bill black with tan band; white back with black and tan markings; black chest and white belly; very long tail feathers.
Female: *Winter*: White face, black crown; back brown with black wings; chest brown and white belly.

Voice: Male — call during courtship sounds similar to yodelling. Female — soft grunting and quacking.
Food: Insect larvae, molluscs, crustaceans.

Bufflehead

Bucephala albeola

Observation Calendar

J F M A M J J A S O N D

Male: Small compact duck; black head with large white patch behind the eye; grey bill; black back with white underparts.
Female: Grey-brown overall with smaller white patch behind the eye.

Voice: Mostly quiet. Male whistles. Female quacks.
Food: Small fish, crustaceans, snails and other molluscs.

Common Goldeneye

Bucephala clangula

Size Identification

Foot: Tridactyl

Flying

Observation Calendar
J F M A M J J A S O N D

Feeding

Male: Black/green head with round white patch on cheek, close to black bill; back black with white bars; underside white; orange feet and legs. *In flight*: Large white speculum.
Female: Brown head and light charcoal overall; bill black with yellow patch; white patches on back. Both male and female are stocky with large head.

Voice: Call during courtship *jeeeeent*. Wings whistle when in flight. Female — low grating sound in flight.
Food: Molluscs, crustaceans, aquatic insects.
Nest/Eggs: In tree cavity or built structure, lined with down. 8-12 eggs.

Hooded Merganser

Lophodytes cucullatus

Observation Calendar

J F M A M J J A S O N D

Male: Black crested head with large white patch on back of head behind eye; black bill is long and thin; rust eye; black back with rust sides and white underparts; black band runs down side into chest; white bands on black wings; tail is often cocked. *In flight*: Rapid energetic wing beats.

Female: Grey breast and belly; faint rust on back of crest; wings dark brown.

Voice: Call is low croaking or *gack*.

Food: Small fish, reptiles, crustaceans, molluscs, aquatic insects.

Nest/Eggs: In tree cavity or built structure, lined with grasses and down feathers, occasionally on ground. 9-12 eggs.

Common Merganser

Mergus merganser

Size Identification

Foot: Tridactyl

Flying

Male: Dark green head crested, with red toothed bill slightly hooked at end; white ring around neck connects to white chest and belly; black back and white sides; feet and legs orange.

Female: Brown head and grey-brown back; white chin.

Voice: Male call is *twaang*. Female call is series of hard notes.

Food: Small fish, crustaceans, molluscs.

Nest/Eggs: Built of reeds and grass and lined with down feathers in tree cavity, rock crevice, on ground or in built structure. 8-11 eggs.

Feeding

Egg: Actual Size

Red-breasted Merganser

Mergus serrator

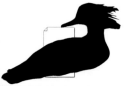

Observation Calendar

J F M A M J J A S O N D

Male: *Winter*: Dark green and black head with crest; red eye; white neck ring; long orange toothed bill with slight hook at end; chest white, spotted black; back black with white patching. *Summer*: Head chestnut brown; overall body grey. *In flight*: Rapid wing beats; straight flying pattern; dark breast on male.

Female: Brown head with grey upper parts and white belly.

Voice: Call for male is *eoooow* usually during courtship. Female — series of hard notes. Mostly quiet.
Food: Small fish, molluscs, crustaceans.
Nest/Eggs: Built of grass and down, in sheltered area under bush. 8-10 eggs.

Ruddy Duck

Oxyura jamaicensis

Size Identification

Foot: Tridactyl

Flying

Feeding

Observation Calendar

J F M A M J J A S O N D

Male: Distinct broad light blue bill; black cap running down back of neck; white cheeks; reddish-brown body; long black tail that is often held upright.
Female: Overall brown with white cheeks; buff line just below eyes; beak is black.

Voice: Mostly quiet except for drumming and clicking sounds by male during courting.
Food: Aquatic plants, crustaceans, aquatic insects.
Nest/Eggs: Floating nest of dry plant material, lined with down and hidden amongst reeds. 6-20 eggs.

Egg: Actual Size

Foot: Tridactyl

Flying

Double-crested Cormorant

Phalacrocorax auritus

Observation Calendar

J F M A M J J A S O N D

Male/Female: Overall black with long tail feathers; bright orange chin and throat patch; feet and legs black. Crest is visible only during courtship. *In flight*: Neck is kinked. Often seen flying extremely high.

Feeding

Did you know? Cormorants are often seen perched on a rock or pier with wings fully extended to dry their feathers.

Voice: Call is a variety of grunts and croaks, only at its nest. Elsewhere silent.
Food: Small fish.
Nest/Eggs: Colonies. Platform built of sticks and twigs, lined with leaves and grass and placed on ground or small tree. 3-5 eggs.

Egg: Actual Size

American Bittern

Botaurus lentiginosus

Size Identification

Foot: Anisodactyl

Flying

Feeding

Observation Calendar

J F M A M J J A S O N D

Male/Female: Overall reddish brown with white stripes on underside; yellow bill long and sharp; short brown tail lightly banded; smudgy brown back. *In flight*: Tips of wings dark brown.

Did you know? The American Bittern is extremely difficult to spot in the field because, if approached, it will freeze and blend into the reeds.

Voice: In flight, a loud *squark*. Song is a loud *kong-chu-chunk*, on breeding grounds.
Food: Small fish, reptiles, amphibians, insects, small mammals.
Nest/Eggs: Concealed platform built from aquatic plants just above water. 2-6 eggs.

Egg: Actual Size

61

Least Bittern

Ixobrychus exilis

Size Identification

Foot: Anisodactyl

Flying

Observation Calendar
J F M A M J J A S O N D

Feeding

Male: Black crown and back; long sharp yellow bill; white chin, chest and belly with reddish tints on sides; dark yellow feet and legs.
Female: Dark crown.

Did you know? You will seldom see a Least Bittern — it is very shy and secretive. If approached it will freeze in position.

Food: Small fish, reptiles.
Voice: Call is sharp *keeek* repeated. Song is soft *kuuu*.
Nest/Eggs: Platform nest built of sticks with grass on top, hidden amongst water plants. 2-7 eggs.

Egg: Actual Size

62

Great Blue Heron

Ardea herodias

Size Identification

Foot: Anisodactyl

Flying

Feeding

Observation Calendar

J F M A M J J A S O N D

Male/Female: Overall grey-blue with black crest on top of head; long neck and bill; black patch connecting eye and long yellow bill; white head; long grey legs and feet; long feathers extend over wings and base of neck. *In flight*: Neck is kinked; legs extend past tail; constant wing flapping with occasional glide.

Voice: Bill makes clacking sound. Call is harsh *squawk*.
Food: Small fish, reptiles, amphibians, crustaceans, birds, aquatic insects.
Nest/Eggs: Colonies. Platform of aquatic plants and twigs, lined with softer materials such as down and soft grass, placed in tree or shrub. 3-7 eggs.

Egg: Actual Size

63

Great Egret

Ardea alba

Observation Calendar

J F M A M J J A S O N D

Male/Female: Overall large white bird; long sharp yellow bill; long black legs and feet; long thin neck; small head; thin feathers off tail; bright yellow eyes.

Did you know? During courtship Great Egrets will clack their bills together while making various head movements and dancing.

Voice: Series of low-pitched *coos*.
Food: Fish, amphibians, insects, small mammals.
Nest/Eggs: Platform nest poorly built of twigs and sticks, in trees or large bushes. Occasionally built in cattails. 1-6 eggs.

Green Heron

Butorides virescens

Observation Calendar

J F M A M J J A S O N D

Male/Female: Distinct reddish-brown cheeks, neck, chest and belly; black cap; black wings with thin white streaking; broad sharp black bill with slight amounts of yellow; yellow eye; feet and legs yellow or orange; white patch above eye and running along base of bill.

Did you know? The Green Heron has been observed placing a twig on the water as bait for prey. When prey approaches the twig the heron strikes quickly with its sharp bill.

Voice: Typical call is sharp *kiew*. When aggressive will call *raah*.
Food: Fish, insects, small amphibians, crabs.
Nest/Eggs: Flat nest built of twigs and sticks, placed in tree or bush. 3-6 eggs.

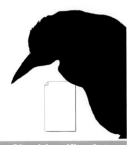

Black-crowned Night Heron

Nycticorax nycticorax

Observation Calendar

J F M A M J J A S O N D

Male/Female: Adult has dark grey upperparts; middle grey wings; light grey chin, chest and belly; black cap; broad sharp black bill; short yellow legs and feet; red eye. Immature is heavily streaked with brown.

Did you know? During breeding dances the two birds extend their necks horizontally and raise their head feathers, while gently touching bills together.

Food: Fish, amphibians, insects, small mammals, occasionally young birds.
Voice: Very rough-sounding low *quok*, usually at dusk. *Roc roc* sound while nesting.
Nest/Eggs: Flat nest built of twigs and aquatic plants then lined with finer plant materials, placed high in shrub or tree. Occasionally on the ground. 3-5 eggs.

Virginia Rail

Rallus limicola

Size Identification

Foot: Anisodactyl

Flying

Feeding

Observation Calendar

J F M A M J J A S O N D

Male/Female: Chicken-like; grey head banded dark charcoal on top; eye red; neck and sides rich rust; long curved red and black bill; back dark brown with rust edging; wings rust with black; short black and brown tail; legs and feet red; belly black and white banding.

Voice: Call is descending *kicket* repeated with grunting notes.
Food: Marine worms, snails, aquatic insects.
Nest/Eggs: Cup of grass and reeds built slightly above water's surface, attached to reeds and other aquatic plant life. 5-12 eggs.

Egg: Actual Size

Sora
Porzana carolina

Size Identification

Foot: Anisodactyl

Flying

Observation Calendar

J F M A M J J A S O N D

Feeding

Male/Female: Chicken-like; grey above eye runs down to chin, breast and belly; black mask behind thick yellow bill; upper parts chestnut brown with white and dark brown bars; legs and feet yellow; buff rump.

Did you know? The Sora, like other rails, prefers to migrate at night.

Voice: Call is musical *kuur weeee,* which is repeated and descends.
Food: Aquatic insects, seeds.
Nest/Eggs: Built in open marsh, attached to reeds, using leaves and grass. 6-15 eggs.

Egg: Actual Size

Common Moorhen

Gallinula chloropus

Size Identification

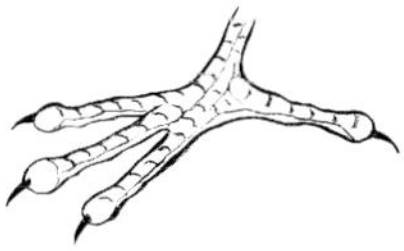

Foot: Anisodactyl

Flying

Feeding

Egg: Actual Size

Observation Calendar

J F M A M J J A S O N D

Male/Female: *Summer*: Overall dark body; bright red forehead and bill; yellow bill tip; white tail feathers at rump; white line of feathers along wing edge; large yellow feet and legs. *Winter*: Red forehead and bill become brownish-yellow.

Did you know? If broods are born close together the first brood will often help with the feeding of the second.

Voice: Similar to chicken clucks, but also makes a variety of sounds including short gravelly noises.
Food: Grasses, seeds, snails, aquatic insects, land insects.
Nest/Eggs: Platform nest built from grasses, over water and attached to aquatic plants. 4-17 eggs.

American Coot
Fulica americana

Size Identification

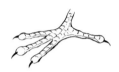

Foot: Anisodactyl

Flying

Observation Calendar
J F M A M J J A S O N D

Male/Female: Duck-like body, slate-coloured overall; white bill and frontal shield shows red swelling at close range; partial black ring around tip of beak; feet and legs greenish-yellow; lobed toes.

Feeding

Did you know? The American Coot has many different courtship displays, including running over the surface of water with its neck and head bent very low.

Voice: Variety of calls including clucks, grunts and other harsh notes and toots sounding like a small trumpet.
Food: Seeds, leaves, roots, small aquatic plants.
Nest/Eggs: Floating platform nest of dead leaves and stems, lined with finer material and anchored to reeds. 8-10 eggs.

Egg: Actual Size

Sandhill Crane
Grus canadensis

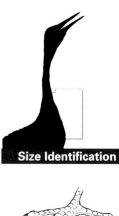

Size Identification

Foot: Anisodactyl

Flying

Feeding

Observation Calendar
J F M A M J J A S O N D

Male/Female: Overall white; dark red patch on forehead; long neck; long sharp black bill; some feathers on back may have rust colouring; tail feathers droop down at end; long legs and feet yellow.

Did you know? The Sandhill Crane has a very elaborate courtship display, with leaps in the air and dancing movements.

Voice: Loud resonant rolling bugle.
Food: Seeds, grains, small mammals, reptiles, frogs, insects.
Nest/Eggs: Large platform nest built of grasses, twigs, aquatic plants and weeds, on ground or possibly in shallow water. 1-3 eggs.

Egg: 80%

Black-bellied Plover
Pluvialis squatarola

Size Identification

Foot: Anisodactyl

Flying

Feeding

Observation Calendar
J F M A M J J A S O N D

Male/Female: *Summer*: Black mask set against pale grey speckled head, crown and neck; bill black; breast and belly black; wings and tail black with white speckles; white rump; feet and legs black. *Winter*: Black face patch; dull grey-brown chest and belly. *In flight*: Black on inner wings underparts; white wing band; white rump.

Voice: Call is whistled three-note *pee oo ee*.
Food: Worms, insects, crustaceans, molluscs, seeds.

Semipalmated Plover

Charadrius semipalmatus

Foot: Anisodactyl

Flying

Feeding

Observation Calendar
J F M A M J J A S O N D

Male/Female: *Summer*: Dark brown head, back and wings; small white patch on forehead with black band above; faint white eyebrow; white chin extending into white collar with black collar band below; chest and belly white; wing feathers black; feet and legs orange; bill is orange, tipped in black. *In flight*: Quick wingbeats with slight glide just before landing.

Voice: Whistle *chee-weee* with a defensive call in quick short notes. Also soft rattling.
Food: Marine worms.
Nest/Eggs: Hollow on ground with shell bits and grass, on sand or gravel. 4 eggs.

73

Killdeer

Charadrius vociferus

Foot: Anisodactyl

Flying

Observation Calendar
J F M A M J J A S O N D

Feeding

Male/Female: Bright red eye with black band running across forehead; white chin, collar and eyebrow; black collar ring under white; black chest band set against white chest and belly; back and wing rust and grey; wing tipped in black; legs and feet pink/grey. *In flight:* Orange rump; black wing tips and white band on trailing edge.

Did you know? A killdeer will exhibit a "broken-wing" display when a predator comes close to the nest sight. The bird will appear hurt and run around distracting the predator from the nest.

Voice: Variety of calls with most common being *kill deeee* which is repeated.
Food: Insects.
Nest/Eggs: Hollow on ground with some pebbles. Most popular sightings in gravel parking lots. 3-4 eggs.

Egg: Actual Size

Greater Yellowlegs

Tringa melanoleuca

Observation Calendar

J F M A M J J A S O N D

Male/Female: Speckled grey and white overall; long bright yellow legs and feet; long straight black bill; short tail feathers with black banding; white belly.

Voice: Call is whistled musical *whew* repeated and descending.
Food: Fish, snails, insects, plants.
Nest/Eggs: Hollow on ground in damp area. 4 eggs.

Lesser Yellowlegs

Tringa flavipes

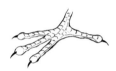

Observation Calendar

J F M A M J J A S O N D

Male/Female: Long black bill; dark upperparts speckled white; white belly; wings and tail feathers banded black; long yellow legs and feet.

Voice: Call is *tu* repeated.

Food: Insects, worms, snails, berries, small fish.

Solitary Sandpiper
Tringa solitaria

Observation Calendar

J F M A M J J A S O N D

Male/Female: *Summer*: Overall dark brown with white spotting; streaked head and neck; white eye ring; long thin black bill; feet and legs dark grey; white belly and rump. *Winter*: Grey overall.

Voice: A series of three high-pitched notes *wheet wheet wheet*.
Food: Aquatic insects, crustaceans, insects, worms.

Spotted Sandpiper
Actitis macularia

Size Identification

Foot: Anisodactyl

Flying

Observation Calendar

J F M A M J J A S O N D

Feeding

Male/Female: *Summer:* Grey-brown on head, back and wings; white eyebrow and black line running from beak to back of neck; long orange bill; white chin, chest and belly with distinct charcoal spots; yellow feet and legs; bobbing tail.
Winter: White underparts — no spots. *In flight:* Quick stiff wingbeats, slightly arched back.

Voice: Quiet bird but makes a *peeetaawet* call during courtship and a whistle that is repeated when alarmed.
Food: Insects, worms, crustaceans, fish, flies, beetles.
Nest/Eggs: Shallow depression on ground, lined with grasses and mosses. 4 eggs.

Egg: Actual Size

Upland Sandpiper
Bartramia longicauda

Size Identification

Foot: Anisodactyl

Flying

Feeding

Observation Calendar

J F M A M J J A S O N D

Male/Female: Brown mottled overall; white belly; small head with long yellow and black bill; long neck and tail feathers; feet and legs yellow.

Did you know? Courtship dances include aerial and ground displays with occasional motions in which the bird holds its wing above its head.

Voice: Call is *pulip pulip* while in flight. Song is lilting double whistle, ascends then descends.
Food: Insects, worms.
Nest/Eggs: Depression in ground lined with fine grasses, in grassy areas such as fields or meadows. 4 eggs.

Egg: Actual Size

Whimbrel

Numenius phaeopus

Size Identification

Foot: Anisodactyl

Flying

Feeding

Observation Calendar

J F M A M J J A S O N D

Male/Female: Overall grey and brown speckled with cream; sides banded with dark brown; long downward curving black bill with yellow underside; cream eyebrow extending from bill; dark brown cap; feet and legs grey; tail brown with dark brown banding.

Voice: Inflight call is rapid *qui* repeated numerous times with no change in pitch.

Food: Insects, marine worms, crustaceans, mollusks, crabs, berries.

Ruddy Turnstone

Arenaria interpres

Size Identification

Foot: Anisodactyl

Flying

Feeding

Observation Calendar

J F M A M J J A S O N D

Male/Female: *Winter*: Speckled brown back, head and wings; white belly, brown bib and white patch on either side; feet and legs dark orange. *Summer*: Overall upperparts brown and black; brown and black bill with white patch just behind bill; black bib with white patch; short black tail. *In flight*: White bands on wings and back.

Did you know? The Ruddy Turnstone got its name because of its feeding habits. The bird wanders down the feeding area turning over stones.

Voice: Call is *tuc e tuc*.
Food: Insects, molluscs, crustaceans, marine worms.

Red Knot
Calidris canutus

Size Identification

Foot: Anisodactyl

Flying

Observation Calendar

J F M A M J J A S O N D

Feeding

Male/Female: *Winter*: Face, neck and chest turn from brick red in summer to light grey; wings and tail turn dark; black bill; legs and feet charcoal.

Did you know? Red Knots are mostly seen flying in flocks of hundreds of birds with Dunlins, plovers, Godwits, sandpipers and many other shorebirds in their migration south or north.

Voice: Call is low *nuuuut*. Soft *currret* in flight.
Food: Molluscs, worms, insects, crabs, seeds.

Sanderling

Calidris alba

Size Identification

Foot: Anisodactyl

Flying

Feeding

Observation Calendar

J F M A M J J A S O N D

Male/Female: *Summer*: Bright brown and speckled on head, back and breast; black tail; white belly; long bill is dark brown; feet and legs black. *Winter*: Light grey head, neck and chest; white cheeks, white belly; tail black. *In flight*: White on underwing; white bar on top side of wing.

Voice: Call is *kip* in flight. Chattering during feeding.
Food: Crustaceans, molluscs, marine worms, insects.

Semipalmated Sandpiper

Calidris pusillus

Observation Calendar

J F M A M J J A S O N D

Male/Female: Short, straight black bill; back is grey-brown; white underparts; black legs with slightly webbed front toes. In winter, uniformly grey on back. *In flight*: Distinctive formations of thousands of birds stretching hundreds of metres, showing white underparts in unison.

Voice: Continuous quavering *churrrk*.
Food: Small marine invertebrates, usually on mud flats.

Least Sandpiper

Calidris minutilla

Foot: Anisodactyl

Flying

Feeding

Observation Calendar

J F M A M J J A S O N D

Male/Female: Long downward curved black bill; overall brown and black; belly and rump white; feet and legs are yellow. Overall colour turns grey in non-breeding seasons. *In flight*: V-shaped wings white on undersides.

Voice: High pitched *kreeeep* rising up. When in flock it gives high repeated notes.

Food: Insects, mollusks, crustaceans, marine worms.

Pectoral Sandpiper
Calidris melanotos

Size Identification

Foot: Anisodactyl

Flying

Observation Calendar

J F M A M J J A S O N D

Male/Female: Overall dark brown with lighter buff trimming feathers; long thin bill dark grey with slight amount of orange, dipping slightly at tip; chest with dense brown streaking on white; belly and rump white; feet and legs greyish-yellow.

Feeding

Did you know? During the mating season males pump up an air sack in the neck for a flight display to attract females.

Voice: In flight call is low hard *churrk*. Male mating call in flight similar to *ooo-ah*, repeated two or three times.
Food: Insects, worms, crabs, grass seeds.

Dunlin

Calidris alpina

Observation Calendar

J F M A M J J A S O N D

Male/Female: Long black bill; grey face with rust and black speckled crown; breast white speckled brown; dull brown wings and back; short black tail; feet and legs black. *In flight*: White underparts and wing feathers.

Did you know? Dunlins usually flock together performing wonderful aerial shows when flushed.

Voice: In flight call: soft *creeeep* or *chit-lit*.
Food: Crustaceans, molluscs, marine worms, insects.

Short-billed Dowitcher

Limnodromus griseus

Observation Calendar

J F M A M J J A S O N D

Male/Female: *Summer:* Rust neck and chest speckled black; back and wings dark brown speckled with buff; dark brown cap on head. *Winter:* Grey speckled overall with dark, barred flanks; black bill fading to yellow near base, white eyebrows; black and brown tail feathers; feet and legs yellow.

Voice: Call is *tu*, repeated several times in soft high-pitch.
Food: Marine worms, molluscs, insects.

Wilson's Snipe

Gallinago delicata

Size Identification

Foot: Anisodactyl

Flying

Feeding

Observation Calendar
J F M A M J J A S O N D

Male/Female: Very long narrow bill; small head and large brown/black eye; buff eye ring; black and white bars on white belly; brown back striped with pale yellow; short yellow feet and legs; tail has rust band. *In flight*: Pointed wings; flies in back and forth motion with quick wingbeats.

Did you know? The Wilson's Snipe uses its long bill to hunt in bog-like conditions where it can penetrate through the soft ground to catch prey below the surface.

Voice: Call is a *swheet swheet* with sharp *scaip* call when flushed.
Food: Larvae, crayfish, molluscs, insects, frogs, seeds.
Nest/Eggs: Hollow in marsh area, concealed with grass, leaves, twigs and moss. 4 eggs.

Egg: Actual Size

American Woodcock
Scolopax minor

Size Identification

Foot: Anisodactyl

Flying

Observation Calendar
J F M A M J J A S O N D

Feeding

Male/Female: Distinctive long, straight, narrow bill of light brown; large brown eyes set back on the head; overall brown-black back with buff underside; feet and legs pale pink. *In flight*: Short wings explode with clatter.

Did you know? When courtship is taking place, the males will rise up in the air and circle around as high as 15 metres.

Voice: A deep *peeeeint* and a tin whistle sounding twitter when in flight.
Food: Earthworms, a variety of insects and insect larvae, seeds.
Nest/Eggs: Shallow depression on ground, lined with dead leaves and needles, in wooded area. 4 eggs.

Egg: Actual Size

Wilson's Phalarope
Phalaropus tricolor

Size Identification

Foot: Anisodactyl

Flying

Observation Calendar
J F M A M J J A S O N D

Observation Calendar
J F M A M J J A S O N D

Male: *Summer*: White throat; light rust on back of head changing to pale grey on breast; pale grey underparts; grey back and wings.

Female: *Summer*: Long thin black bill, white chin and cheeks turning rust running down white neck; black band runs from beak through eye down side of neck to back; grey cap; white sides and belly; grey feet and legs. *In flight*: White rump; no wing bands; long legs.

Male/Female: *Winter*: Similar to summer male with pale grey, not rust, on head and neck.

Feeding

Did you know? This is one species where the male does all the nest tending. He builds the nest, incubates eggs and raises young.

Voice: Soft call is *aangh*.
Food: Insects, crustaceans.

Red-necked Phalarope

Phalaropus lobatus

Size Identification

Foot: Anisodactyl

Flying

Observation Calendar

J F M A M J J A S O N D

Feeding

Male/Female: *Winter*: White and grey chest and belly. Face white with black mark behind eye; dark grey wings and back.
Male: *Summer:* Top of head black; long black bill; white chin; black band running under eye against white and rust; rust neck; grey chest changing to white belly; dark brown and rust wings and back; tail black; white rump.
Female: Overall similar markings except bolder colour; rufous neck with more contrast overall.

Voice: Call is sharp *twic*.
Food: Aquatic insects, molluscs, crustaceans.

Bonaparte's Gull
Larus philadelphia

Foot: Tridactyl

Flying

Observation Calendar

J F M A M J J A S O N D

Male/Female: *Summer*: Smaller gull with dark head and bill; white neck, chest and belly; grey back and black tail feathers. *Winter*: During winter months black cap disappears and a small black spot on side of head turns white. *In flight*: Wings appear black tipped.

Voice: Low rasping *gerrrr* or *wreeeek*.
Food: Small fish, worms, ground insects.

Feeding

93

Ring-billed Gull
Larus delawarensis

Observation Calendar
J F M A M J J A S O N D

Male/Female: *Summer*: White overall; yellow bill with black band at end; yellow eye; pale grey wings and black tips and white patches within black tips; black feet and legs. *Winter*: Feet and legs turn yellow; light brown spots on top of head and back of neck. *In flight*: Grey underparts; black wing tips.

Voice: Loud *kaawk* and other calls.
Food: Insects, bird eggs, worms, garbage.
Nest/Eggs: Colonies. Grasses, sticks, twigs and pebbles, built on ground. 3 eggs.

Herring Gull

Larus argentatus

Observation Calendar

J F M A M J J A S O N D

Male/Female: White head that in winter is streaked light brown; yellow eye and bill; small red patch on lower bill; tail black; feet and legs red. *In flight:* Grey wing with white on trailing edge and black tips; pale brown rump; wide charcoal tail feathers.

Voice: Variety of squawks and squeals. Aggressive alarm call is *kak kak kak kak* ending in *yucca*.
Food: Insects, small mammals, clams, fish, small birds, crustaceans, mussels, rodents, garbage.
Nest/Eggs: Colonies. Mound lined with grass and seaweed on ground or cliff. Usually on islands. 2-4 eggs.

Iceland Gull

Larus glaucoides kumlieni

Size Identification

Foot: Tridactyl

Flying

Observation Calendar
J F M A M J J A S O N D

Male/Female: Overall white with light grey back and wings; white wings underside; yellow bill with red tip on lower part; yellow eye; dark pink feet and legs. *In flight:* Overall white and grey underparts; white patches on wing tips.

Feeding

Voice: Mostly quiet. Variety of squeaks.
Food: Fish, carrion, bird eggs.

Glaucous Gull

Larus hyperboreus

Size Identification

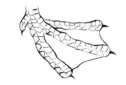

Foot: Tridactyl

Flying

Feeding

Observation Calendar

J F M A M J J A S O N D

Male/Female: Overall white with light grey back and wings; bill is yellow with red patch on lower portion at tip; yellow eye; pink legs and feet; short square white tail. *In flight*: White wing tips on grey wings.

Voice: Variety of squawks and other calls that are deep and hoarse sounding.

Food: Small mammals, birds, eggs, insects, garbage, small fish, crustaceans, carrion, molluscs.

Great Black-backed Gull

Larus marinus

Observation Calendar

J F M A M J J A S O N D

Male/Female: White head, chin, chest and belly; red patch on lower portion of bill; feet and legs pink/grey; black wings with thin white band on trailing edge; tail and back black.
In flight: Pale grey undersides with black wing tips; tail white.

Voice: Loud squawks and deep guttural notes.
Food: Scavenger. Small fish, mammals, young birds and garbage. Major predator of other birds including puffin and tern chicks.
Nest/Eggs: Colonies. Mound of seaweed and other coastal plants, lined with grasses, on ground or rocky ledge. 3 eggs.

Caspian Tern

Sterna caspia

Foot: Tridactyl

Flying

Feeding

Observation Calendar

J F M A M J J A S O N D

Male/Female: Largest tern, with distinctive black cap; long sharp orange bill; white neck, chest and belly; grey back with long grey wings; short white tail; feet black. Juvenile feet often yellow.

Voice: Deep heronlike *aayayam* and harsh *cahar*.
Food: Small fish.
Nest/Eggs: Mostly nests in colonies. Nest is a depression in ground, lined with grass and seaweed, on a sandy beach. 2-3 eggs.

Egg: 85%

Common Tern
Sterna hirundo

Size Identification

Foot: Tridactyl

Flying

Observation Calendar

J F M A M J J A S O N D

Feeding

Male/Female: *Summer*: Soft grey overall with black cap; white cheeks; long thin red bill with black tip; short red feet and legs; wings and tail feathers grey, exceptionally long; white underside to tail. *Winter*: Black cap recedes leaving white face; black bar on wing; charcoal on tail. *In flight*: Charcoal on wing tips; grey overall; quick wingbeats.

Voice: Short *kip* repeated and louder *keeeear.*
Food: Small fish.
Nest/Eggs: Colonies. On ground, cup of grasses on sandy or pebbled areas. Most often on islands. 2-3 eggs.

Egg: Actual Size

Forster's Tern
Sterna forsteri

Observation Calendar
J F M A M J J A S O N D

Male: Overall white body with grey wings; distinct black cap; bright orange-red bill with black tip; grey and white tail extends slightly beyond folded wings; feet and legs orange.

Voice: Short calls including *keeer*, *zreeep* and *kip*.
Food: Fish, flying insects.
Nest/Eggs: Cavity scraped into ground on sandy or gravel beaches, often on islands. 3-4 eggs.

Black Tern

Childonius niger

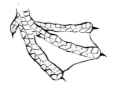

Observation Calendar
J F M A M J J A S O N D

Male/Female: *Summer*: Black head, bill, chest and belly; white rump; feet and legs black; wings and tail charcoal. *Winter*: Wings and back charcoal; head white with black on top; white chest and underparts.

Did you know? This is one very fast bird. The Black Tern catches insects in flight.

Voice: Call is short *kirc* of *keeeel*.
Food: Insects.
Nest: Colonies. Loosely built pile of aquatic plants and grasses, on water's edge or floating on water. 3 eggs.

Land Birds

Many of the land birds described in the following pages can be seen anywhere in the southern part of Ontario. In woodlands and meadows, where songbirds and other small species such as chickadees, finches, flycatchers, nuthatches, sparrows and warblers abound, you are also likely to see hawks and other raptors.

In wilderness areas where habitat is less disturbed by human activity — especially in national and provincial parks — there are opportunities to see and hear some less common species. Park interpreters can provide specific information on the birds and hot spot areas to be found in each park.

Many species have adapted well to urban settings. In parks and suburban neighbourhoods, you can see a wide variety of year-round inhabitants. Birds can be attracted to your backyard by the type of tree, bushes and plants that are growing there. This book indicates those that will come to your backyard bird feeder and those that will make use of a nesting box. Each bird requires a different type of nesting box and you can learn more about making these by visiting birding web sites.

The visual keys in this section depict seasonal range - when you will see the bird - its size, the type of foot and the nesting location. The egg is shown for birds that breed in the province. The description emphasizes the distinctive markings of each bird, the food preferences and the calls or songs of each bird.

Size Identification

Foot: Anisodactyl

Egg: 60%

Turkey Vulture
Cathartes aura

Observation Calendar
J F M A M J J A S O N D

Male/Female: Large overall black bird; silver-grey underside of wings is seen in flight; naked red head; pale yellow sharply curved beak; feet and legs charcoal.

Did you know? Turkey vultures are most commonly seen soaring high over the countryside with their long wings held upward in a wide V-shape.

Voice: Grunts and hisses during aggression or feeding.
Food: Carrion.
Nest/Eggs: Nest made of scrap on ground, usually in cave, on cliff, hollow of tree or in fallen log. 1-3 eggs.

Nesting Location

Osprey

Pandion haliaetus

Size Identification

Foot: Anisodactyl

Egg: 70%

Male/Female: In flight: White belly and chest; wings grey with black banding; white wing underparts connect to chest; black band running through eye; large black bill; tail grey with black banding. **Perched**: Black back and wings with thin white line running above wing; eye yellow with black band running through and down to cheek; chin white; top of head white with black patches.

Female: More streaked then male.

Voice: A loud chirp which trails off or ascending **squeeeee** during courtship displays.

Food: Various small fish.

Nest/Eggs: Constructed of twigs and sticks, lined with sod, grass and vines, in upper parts of trees and on top of poles, 60 feet above ground. 2-3 eggs.

Nesting Location

Bald Eagle

Haliaeetus leucocephalus

Size Identification

Foot: Anisodactyl

Egg: 70%

Observation Calendar

J F M A M J J A S O N D

Male/Female: In flight: Broad black wings and belly with white head and tail feathers. **Perched**: White head with brilliant yellow eyes; white tail feathers; black back and wings; feet and legs yellow; bill yellow.

Juvenile: Mistaken for Golden Eagle because it lacks white head and tail; chest white and speckled; black wings with white speckles; underparts black with large areas of white.

Did you know? The eagle population is now recovering from rapid declines in the 1970s due to the widespread use of DDT.

Voice: A loud scream given in multiples.
Food: A variety of small and medium-sized mammals, fish and carrion.
Nest/Eggs: Upper parts of large, often dead, trees built with large twigs, lined with grass, moss, sod and weeds. 2 eggs.

Nesting Location

Northern Harrier (Marsh Hawk)

Circus cyaneus

Size Identification

Foot: Anisodactyl

Egg: 90%

Observation Calendar

Male: In flight: White underside with black and rust speckles; head is grey; black on tips of wings; orange feet; wings are V-shaped in flight. **Perched:** Grey head with white face mask; yellow eyes; thin rust banding down front; white rump.
Female: Slightly larger than male with brown overall; buff face disk around cheeks; buff under chin and belly is banded with brown; bill grey; yellow eyes.

Did you know? While gliding over meadows, the Northern Harrier's wings take a V-shape, making it easy to identify.

Voice: Relatively quiet bird with occasional screams of alarm.
Food: A variety of small mammals and birds.
Nest/Eggs: On or near ground, built of sticks, straw and grasses. 4-5 eggs.

Nesting Location

Sharp-shinned Hawk
Accipiter striatus

Size Identification

Foot: Anisodactyl

Egg: Actual Size

Observation Calendar
J F M A M J J A S O N D

Male/Female: **In flight**: Small hawk with rust chest banded with buff; long square tail is white with charcoal banding; wings dark brown and rounded; top of head dark brown. **Perched**: Brick-red eyes with brown band just below eye; bill is black with yellow base; feet and legs yellow; white feathers extend out of rust-coloured belly.

Did you know? Over the past few years there has been a dramatic decrease in the eastern population. This may be directly related to the decrease in songbirds that it hunts.

Voice: A quick high pitched **kik kik kik.**
Food: Small songbirds.
Nest/Eggs: Broad platforms of twigs and sticks in conifers or deciduous trees built against the trunk, lined with bark. 4-5 eggs.

Nesting Location

108

Cooper's Hawk

Accipiter cooperii

Size Identification

Foot: Anisodactyl

Egg: Actual Size

Observation Calendar

J F M A M J J A S O N D

Male/Female: In flight: White chest and belly with rust banding down to lower belly; buff tail is long and rounded with faint charcoal banding; chin white; buff and white under wings with charcoal banding; grey on top of head. When in flight it has a steady wingbeat. **Perched**: Grey wings and tail with rust edging at ends; eyes are brick red; bill black and yellow; feet and legs yellow with rust feathers banded white down to knee.

Voice: Call is a loud **kek kek kek**.
Food: Small birds.
Nest/Eggs: Large nest built of sticks and twigs, in conifer tree, 6-18 metres above ground. 4-5 eggs.

Nesting Location

Northern Goshawk

Accipiter gentilis

Size Identification

Foot: Anisodactyl

Egg: 80%

Observation Calendar

J F M A M J J A S O N D

Male/Female: In flight: Underside is grey with dark brown banding overall; tail long with rich red along edges; buff eyebrow runs to back of neck. **Perched**: Dark brown wings with buff edging; eye brick red; bill black with yellow at base; feet and legs yellow with white feathers, banded brown reaching down to knees.

Did you know? This is an aggressive bird that has the ability to fly in densely wooded areas chasing small birds.

Voice: Loud **keeek keeek keeek**.
Food: Small birds and occasional small mammals, such as squirrels.
Nest/Eggs: Stick nest lodged in crotch of tree against the trunk, lined with bark, feathers and down. 3-4 eggs.

Nesting Location

Red-shouldered Hawk

Buteo lineatus

Size Identification

Foot: Anisodactyl

Egg: 60%

Observation Calendar

J F M A M J J A S O N D

Male/Female: In flight: Rust-red chest lightly banded with buff; pale crescent on outer area of wings. **Perched**: Red brick shoulder patch; black wings with streaks of white; head buff with dark brown streaking; tail dark with white banding; bill black with yellow at base; feet and legs yellow with buff feathers banded with rust that reach just above feet; eyes dark.

Did you know? Red-shouldered Hawks return to the same nesting site year after year.

Voice: Decreasing scream **ke-er-ke-er-ke-er.**
Food: Amphibians, snakes, small mammals, small birds, insects.
Nest/Eggs: Sticks and twigs lined with bark, feathers and down, built close to trunk in cavity of tree, near swamps and bogs. 3 eggs.

111

Nesting Location

Broad-winged Hawk

Buteo platypterus

Size Identification

Foot: Anisodactyl

Egg: 75%

Observation Calendar

J F M A M J J A S O N D

Male/Female: In flight: Brownish-red banding on chest and belly; wings white with faint banding; tail broad with large black banding against white; chin white; top of head brown. **Perched**: Dark brown wings; yellow eye ringed in black; feet and legs yellow; bill charcoal grey.

Did you know? In September hawks sometimes gather together in flocks of hundreds.

Voice: Whistle that is high-pitched **peee peeeeee**.
Food: Small mammals, birds, reptiles, amphibians.
Nest/Eggs: Small stick, twigs and leaves, lined with bark, in main supporting branches of tree, against trunk. 2-3 eggs.

Nesting Location

Red-tailed Hawk

Buteo jamaicensis

Size Identification

Foot: Anisodactyl

Egg: 75%

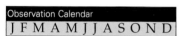

Observation Calendar

J F M A M J J A S O N D

Male/Female: In flight: Tail will appear faint red depending on light; broad wings and belly, white banded with charcoal. **Perched**: Wings are dark brown with buff edges; eyes brick red; bill yellow and black; feet and legs yellow with white feathers banded brown/charcoal reaching to knees; tail brick red.

Voice: A scream that is downward **keeer er er.**
Food: Small mammals, amphibians, nestlings, insects, reptiles, birds.
Nest/Eggs: Flat and shallow, stick and twig nest, lined with moss and evergreen sprigs, on rocky ledges or in trees that are in the open, 10-30 metres above ground. 2 eggs.

Nesting Location

Rough-legged Hawk

Buteo lagopus

Size Identification

Foot: Anisodactyl

Observation Calendar

J F M A M J J A S O N D

Male/Female: In flight: Dark patches on white belly with banding; black patch at wrist of underwing; white tail with one dark band at tip. **Perched**: Dark brown wings with buff head that is banded with dark brown; yellow eyes; base of tail white rump; black bill, yellow at base; yellow feet and legs with buff feathers that are banded brown to knees.

Food: Small rodents.
Voice: A whistle along with a **keeeerrr** that descends.
Nest/Eggs: Stick nest in tree. 2-4 eggs

Nesting Location

114

Golden Eagle
Aquila chrysaetos

Size Identification

Foot: Anisodactyl

Observation Calendar

J F M A M J J A S O N D

Male/Female: Large eagle; warm golden-brown overall; yellow bill darker at tip; yellow feet and legs; very broad dark wings; head extends far out from wing base. **In flight**: Wings slightly V-shaped. Immature has white at base of primaries and tail.

Food: Small mammals such as rabbits and rodents. Occasionally birds such as ducks and geese.
Voice: Chirps repeatedly near food, otherwise quiet.

Nesting Location

American Kestrel
Falco sparverius

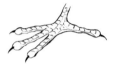

Observation Calendar
J F M A M J J A S O N D

Male/Female: In flight: Overall buff with black speckles; distinctive black banding on face. **Perched**: charcoal wings with black, separated banding; back rust with black banding; grey top of head with rust patch on top; black bands running down cheeks against white; bill black/charcoal with yellow at base; feet and legs orange; tail deep rust with broad black tip.

Voice: Rapid **klee klee klee** or **kily kily kily.**
Food: Mice, voles, insects, small birds.
Nest/Eggs: In cavity of tree or man-made boxes, little or no nesting material. 3-5 eggs.

Merlin
Falco columbarius

Foot: Anisodactyl

Egg: Actual Size

Observation Calendar
J F M A M J J A S O N D

Male: In flight: Buff underside with dark brown banding overall; dark brown head with thin buff eyebrow; tail dark. **Perched**: Slate-blue wings with slight amount of white edges; bill black with yellow at base; feet and legs pale yellow.
Female: Brown back and wings; buff underparts with brown streaks.

Did you know? Often called the "bullet hawk," this is a very fast bird when racing after its prey. It has a wonderful ability to turn quickly and accelerate in flight, even through thick woods.

Voice: Rapid and high-pitched **clee clee clee.**
Food: Small birds in flight, reptiles, amphibians, insects.
Nest/Eggs: Sticks interwoven with moss, twigs, lichen and conifer needles, on cliff ledge or cavity of tree. 4-5 eggs.

Nesting Location

Peregrine Falcon
Falco peregrinus

Size Identification

Foot: Anisodactyl

Egg: 80%

Male/Female: **In flight**: Overall white underside with charcoal banding; face has black mask and sideburns with yellow around dark eyes; bill is yellow and grey' feet and legs are yellow. **Perched**: Black wings with buff edging on feathers.

Did you know? The Peregrine can reach the fastest speeds of any animal on earth — 260 km/h.

Voice: A series of high pitched screams **ki ki ki.**
Food: Catches birds in flight and occasionally will eat larger insects.
Nest/Eggs: Slight hollow in rock ledge or flat roof top, built with sticks. 3-5 eggs.

Nesting Location

118

Ring-necked Pheasant

Phasianus colchicus

Size Identification

Foot: Anisodactyl

Egg: 90%

Observation Calendar
J F M A M J J A S O N D

Observation Calendar
J F M A M J J A S O N D

Male: Green iridescent head with distinctive red wattles (patches around eye); white collar; overall body is mixture of grey, black and brown; long tail feathers brown with black banding; feet and legs charcoal grey; pale yellow bill.
Female: Grey-brown overall with dark markers over entire body; pale yellow bill; small red wattle above eye.

Did you know? This chicken-like bird gets into some real cock fights in early spring, jumping, pecking, clawing for its right to territory.

Voice: Similar to a wild turkey gobble at a higher pitch.
Food: Seeds, insects, grains, berries.
Nest/Eggs: Shallow bowl on ground, lined with weed, grass and leaves. 6-15 eggs.

Nesting Location

Ruffed Grouse

Bonasa umbellus

Size Identification

Foot: Anisodactyl

Egg: Actual Size

Observation Calendar

J F M A M J J A S O N D

Male: Distinctive crest on head; overall brown speckled bird with black shoulder band on back of neck; tail is grey with broad black band at tip; eye brown; feet and legs grey.
Female: Similar to male except browner and more barring on underside; black shoulder band is narrower.

Did you know? The female will act injured if there is a threat near the nest.

Voice: An alarm note of **qit qit**. Cooing by female.
Food: A variety of insects, seeds, tree buds, leaves and berries.
Nest/Eggs: Hollow under log or near the base of a tree, lined with leaves, pine needles and feathers. 9-12 eggs.

Nesting Location

Wild Turkey

Meleagris gallopavo

Size Identification

Foot: Anisodactyl

Egg: 65%

Observation Calendar
J F M A M J J A S O N D

Male: An extremely large bird; overall dark dusky-brown body; iridescent bronze sheen and banding of reddish-brown, black and white; head is featherless, grey and red; blueish and reddish wattles; tail is fan shaped when open and has chestnut or buff tips; spurs and 'beard' on breast; feet and legs reddish-grey.

Female: Smaller than male and less iridescence; no spurs or 'beard.'

Voice: Gobbling and clucking calls.
Food: Seeds, grains, insects, frogs, lizards, vegetation, nuts.
Nest/Eggs: Scraped depression in ground, lined with leaves and grasses. 6-20 eggs.

Nesting Location

Rock Pigeon

Columba livia

Size Identification

Foot: Anisodactyl

Egg: Actual Size

Observation Calendar
J F M A M J J A S O N D

Male/Female: Varies greatly from solid white to solid black and everything in between. Most birds have dark grey head with hints of iridescent colours along the neck; body light grey with two charcoal wing bands; tail and wings dark grey with black bands; rump is white.

Did you know? Pigeons were introduced to North America in the 1800s. They are now prevalent everywhere, especially in urban areas.

Voice: Soft descending **kooooo kooooo.**
Food: Seeds and grain
Nest/Eggs: Flimsy nest of twigs, grass, straw and debris, on ledges or crevices of buildings and bridges, in colonies. 1-2 eggs.

Nesting Location

122

Mourning Dove
Zenaida macroura

Size Identification

Foot: Anisodactyl

Observation Calendar
J F M A M J J A S O N D

Observation Calendar
J F M A M J J A S O N D

Male: Buff-coloured head and body; dark grey wings and tail; bill is black with speckles of red at opening; wings have small black feathers highlighted against softer grey; eyes black surrounded by light blue; feet and legs red; tail is long and pointed.
Female: Similar except head, neck and chest are evenly brown.

Did you know? When the mourning dove is in flight its wings whistle.

Egg: Actual Size

Backyard Feeder

Voice: Very distinct cooing that sounds a little sad, **coooahooo oo oo oo** fading at the end.
Food: A variety of seeds and grain.
Nest/Eggs: Platform of sticks and twigs, lined with grass and rootlets, in evergreens, 15 metres above ground. 1-2 eggs.

Nesting Location

Black-billed Cuckoo
Coccyzus erythropthalmus

Size Identification

Foot: Anisodactyl

Egg: Actual Size

Observation Calendar
J F M A M J J A S O N D

Male/Female: Distinct black beak curved slightly downward; red ring around black eyes; upper body parts brown; wings brown; long tail with three white spots on underside; white chin, chest and belly; feet and legs charcoal grey.

Did you know? The Black-billed Cuckoo is an important species for farmers since much of its diet consists of caterpillars, which are destructive to plants.

Voice: Softly repeated **cu cu cu cu cu** in groups of two to five at the same pitch.
Food: Insects, lizards, mollusks, fishes, frogs, berries.
Nest/Eggs: Shallow, built of twigs and grasses and lined with softer materials including ferns, roots and plant-down; usually built near tree trunk in dense area. 2-5 eggs.

Nesting Location

Common Barn Owl
Tyto alba

Size Identification

Foot: Zygodactyl

Observation Calendar
J F M A M J J A S O N D

Male/Female: Large heart-shaped white face with reddish-brown trim; overall reddish-brown, light brown and black mottled; neck, chest and belly white with dark streaking; long legs covered in white feathers; feet yellow.

Egg: Actual Size

Did you know? The Common Barn Owl has the most acute hearing of all the owls. In total darkness it can hear mouse footsteps within a 30-metre area. Despite its name, this bird is extremely rare.

Voice: Hissing and screeching sounds with occasional clicks. Mostly quiet unless approached.
Food: Rats, mice, insects, bats, various reptiles.
Nest/Eggs: Cavity nest built in old barns or buildings, or in holes already established by mammals along cliffs or banks. No nest materials. 4-7 eggs.

Birdhouse Nester

Nesting Location

Eastern Screech Owl
Otus asio

Size Identification

Foot: Zygodactyl

Egg: Actual Size

Observation Calendar
J F M A M J J A S O N D

Male/Female: Small owl overall with reddish or grey morphs; large yellow eyes; feet and legs yellow; white chest with dark brown streaking; small ear tufts.

Voice: Ascending winnows or melodic trill at same pitch.
Food: Small mammals, insects, amphibians, small birds.
Nest/Eggs: Cavity nest with no linings. 3-5 eggs.

Birdhouse Nester

Nesting Location

Great Horned Owl
Bubo virginianus

Foot: Zygodactyl

J F M A M J J A S O N D

Male/Female: Very recognizable ear tufts that sit wide apart; bright yellow eyes surrounded by rust colour; grey and brown overall with black bands.

Egg: 80%

Voice: Hoot consists of several **hoo hoo hoo hoo hoo hoo**. Male is deeper then female.
Food: Small mammals, birds, reptiles.
Nest/Eggs: Nests in a deserted hawk's, heron's or crow's nest with very little material added. Occasionally will lay eggs on ground amongst bones, skulls and bits of fur. 1-3 eggs.

Nesting Location

Snowy Owl
Nyctea scandiaca

Size Identification

Foot: Zygodactyl

Observation Calendar

J F M A M J J A S O N D

Male/Female: Short black bill; overall white with brilliant yellow eye; small amount of grey speckling throughout with very faint grey banding on chest and sides; feet are covered in white feathers, with long black claws.

Voice: High-pitched screech in breeding and low muffled hoot repeated.
Food: Small mammals, fish, birds, carrion.
Nest/Eggs: Slight depression on ground lined with moss and grass. 5-7 eggs.

Nesting Location

Barred Owl

Strix varia

Foot: Zygodactyl

Egg: 80%

Observation Calendar

J F M A M J J A S O N D

Male/Female: Large dark eyes set in buff and rich brown; white bands extend out from face, down the back including wings and tail feathers; chest white with rich brown feathers in columns; bill is small, yellow, hook shape.

Did you know? The Barred Owl's ears are positioned differently on either side of the head. This allows for better hearing in total darkness.

Voice: Very rhythmic hoots in series of four or five at a time.
Food: Small mammals
Nest/Eggs: Cavity of tree or abandoned hawk's or crow's nest; no lining added. 2-3 eggs.

Nesting Location

Long-eared Owl
Asio otus

Size Identification

Foot: Zygodactyl

Egg: Actual Size

Observation Calendar
J F M A M J J A S O N D

Male/Female: Overall brown mottled with buff; large yellow eyes surrounded by dark areas; cup on face with white rim; short curved black bill; legs covered in white feathers; feet yellow; light belly with subtle streaking on sides; tufts rarely seen.

Did you know? The Long-eared Owl will live in a small community of other owls during the winter months.

Food: Small mammals but favouring voles. Young owls will hunt songbirds and other game birds.
Voice: Low **hooooo** in a long series of notes. Snarls and squeals if approached during feeding.
Nest/Eggs: Nest in trees 3-10 metres above ground. They will usually use the old nest of a crow, hawk or squirrel. 3-7 eggs.

Nesting Location

130

Short-eared Owl

Asio flammeus

Size Identification

Foot: Zygodactyl

Observation Calendar

J F M A M J J A S O N D

Egg: 70%

Male/Female: Dark brown overall with buff banding on back; small ear tufts black and buff directly above eyes on top of head (rarely seen); wings and tail feathers dark brown with buff bands; light buff chest and belly with brown streaks; long wings tipped black at the ends; eyes brilliant yellow surrounded by black; bill black; feet and legs black.

Did you know? The Short-eared Owl flies low to the ground when hunting but is able to hover momentarily when prey is spotted.

Voice: Raspy **yip yip yip.**
Food: Small mammals, mostly voles, songbirds and game birds.
Nest/Eggs: Slight depression hidden in grass. Lined with grass and feathers. 4-9 eggs.

Nesting Location

Northern Saw-whet Owl

Aegolius acadicus

Size Identification

Foot: Zygodactyl

Egg: Actual Size

Observation Calendar

J F M A M J J A S O N D

Male/Female: Yellow eyes that are surrounded by a reddish-brown facial disk; chest white with brown streaks running length of body; feet and legs grey.

Voice: Whistled song repeated **too too too.**

Food: Diet consists mainly of small mammals, including voles, chipmunks and bats, also insects.

Nest/Eggs: Cavity of dead tree, 4-18 metres above ground. No material added. 2-6 eggs.

Nesting Location

Common Nighthawk

Chordeiles minor

Size Identification

Foot: Anisodactyl

Egg: Actual Size

Observation Calendar

J F M A M J J A S O N D

Male: Grey and black speckled bird with long thin wings; white collar wraps around to bottom of neck; legs and feet light grey. When in flight white bands near tail are visible.

Did you know? This bird eats in flight by scooping insects into its large mouth. You can often see nighthawks feeding near lights on warm nights.

Voice: A nasal sounding *peeent.*
Food: Flying insects.
Nest/Eggs: In depression on the ground, often in gravel, with lining. 2 eggs.

Nesting Location

Whip-poor-will
Caprimulgus vociferus

Size Identification

Foot: Anisodactyl

Egg: Actual Size

Observation Calendar

J F M A M J J A S O N D

Male/Female: Grey fluffy bird with brown cheeks; short black rounded wings; short tail; black bill lightly covered with feathers; large black eyes.

Voice: A series of *whip-poor-will, whip-poor-will* with accent on last word.
Food: Flying insects including moths, beetles and grasshoppers.
Nest/Eggs: Depression of dead leaves on the ground formed around eggs. 2 eggs.

Nesting Location

Chimney Swift

Chaetura pelagica

Size Identification

Foot: Anisodactyl

Observation Calendar
J F M A M J J A S O N D

Male/Female: Dark charcoal on head, back, wings and tail; lighter on chest and throat; black bill is small with light grey on underside; feet and legs grey.

Egg: Actual Size

Did you know? A Chimney Swift is capable of snapping off tree twigs with its feet while in flight. It then takes the twig in its mouth and returns to its nest.

Voice: A very quick and repeated *chitter, chitter, chitter* with occasional *chip.*

Food: Flying insects such as moths and beetles.

Nest/Eggs: Flimsy half cup attached by saliva to crevice or rock ledge in chimneys, barns, old buildings and on rock formations. 3-6 eggs.

Nesting Location

Ruby-throated Hummingbird

Archilochus colubris

Observation Calendar

J F M A M J J A S O N D

Male: Dark green head which is iridescent in parts; red throat begins darker under chin; white collar, breast and belly; wings and notched tail black; iridescent green on back; black bill is long and thin; small white area behind eyes; feet and legs black.
Female: Head, back and parts of tail are bright iridescent green; white throat, chest and belly; wings and tail black with white outer tips; black bill is long and thin; small white area behind eyes; feet and legs black.

Voice: A low *hummmmmmm* followed occasionally by an angry sounding squeak or chattering.
Food: Nectar from a variety of plants including thistles, jewel-weed, trumpet vines and other blossoms, occasionally insects.
Nest/Eggs: Small, tightly woven cup with deep cavity built with fibres and attached with spider web, lined with plant down, covered on the outside with lichens, in tree or shrub, 3-6 metres above ground. 2 eggs.

Belted Kingfisher

Ceryle alcyon

Size Identification

Foot: Anisodactyl

Egg: Actual Size

Observation Calendar

J F M A M J J A S O N D

Male: A large head and long black bill; crested blue/black head; very short blue tail; wings black with white bands; chest white; white collar wraps around neck with blue band that wraps around chest; feet and legs charcoal.

Female: Same as male except a rust-coloured breast band.

Did you know? Belted Kingfishers teach their young to dive for food by catching a fish, stunning it, then placing it on the surface of the water. The young birds then practise diving for it.

Voice: A continuous deep rattle during flight.

Food: Small fish, amphibians, reptiles, insects, crayfish.

Nest/Eggs: A cavity or tunnel excavated in a bank near a river or lake. 5-8 eggs.

Nesting Location

Red-headed Woodpecker

Melanerpes erythrocephalus

Size Identification

Foot: Zygodactyl

Egg: Actual Size

Backyard Feeder

Observation Calendar

J F M A M J J A S O N D

Male/Female: Bright red hood over head with grey and black bill; back is black with large distinctive white patches on wings; feet and legs grey; tail feathers are pointed and black; chest and belly white.

Did you know? These woodpeckers are declining because of forestry practices and are competing unsuccessfully with European starlings for nesting locations.

Voice: Call is a deep hoarse *queer queeeer queeer.*
Food: A variety of insects and insect larvae.
Nest/Eggs: Cavity of tree with no added material, 2-25 metres above ground. 4-7 eggs.

Nesting Location

Red-bellied Woodpecker

Melanerpes carolinus

Observation Calendar
J F M A M J J A S O N D

Male: Bright red cap stretching down back of neck; long sharp black beak; tan chin, chest and belly; short black tail with white stripes; black back with white bands; feet and legs charcoal grey; reddish patch on lower belly seldom visible.
Female: Grey face with red crown running down back of head.

Did you know? The Red-bellied Woodpecker will store food in tree cavities and crevices.

Voice: Harsh *churrrr* and *chuck chuck chuck* descending in pitch. Drums and bursts.
Food: Insects, fruit, seeds, nuts.
Nest/Eggs: Creates cavity in living or nearly dead tree. 3-8 eggs.

Size Identification

Foot: Zygodactyl

Egg: Actual Size

Backyard Feeder

Birdhouse Nester

Nesting Location

Yellow-bellied Sapsucker

Sphyrapicus varius

Size Identification

Foot: Zygodactyl

Observation Calendar

J F M A M J J A S O N D

Egg: Actual Size

Male: Red cap and chin with black outlines; white face with black line running through eye from bill to back of head; centre of belly yellow; feet and legs black.
Female: Chin white, not red.

Backyard Feeder

Voice: Drumming on trees in quick short bursts followed by irregular drumming. Occasional *chuurrrr* or *weep*.
Food: Flying insects, spiders, berries, fruit. Drinks sap from trees.
Nest/Eggs: Cavity builder, often in decaying aspens or other trees. 5-6 eggs.

Nesting Location

140

Downy Woodpecker

Picoides pubescens

Foot: Zygodactyl

Observation Calendar

J F M A M J J A S O N D

Male: Black crown ends in very bright red spot on back of head; white extends from cheeks to lower belly; wings and tail black with white banding; feet and legs grey.
Female: Similar except without red spot on back of head.

Voice: Whiny call and a *queek queek* call during courtship. Listen for bird pounding on trees looking for insects.
Food: Larvae and other tree-dwelling insects.
Nest/Eggs: Cavity for nest excavated in decaying trees, 1-5 metres above ground. 3-6 eggs.

Egg: Actual Size

Backyard Feeder

Nesting Location

Hairy Woodpecker

Picoides villosus

Size Identification

Foot: Zygodactyl

Egg: Actual Size

Backyard Feeder

Observation Calendar

J F M A M J J A S O N D

Male/Female: Black head with white banding along cheek and through eye; white back and underparts; wings and tail black with white spotting; feet and legs charcoal grey; bill is nearly length of head; outer tail feathers white.

Voice: A bright sounding *peek...peek*, which may be followed by a rattling call. *Wickiwickiwicki* call during courtship.
Food: Larvae, wood-boring insects. At feeders suet and wildflower seeds.
Nest/Eggs: Cavity for nest excavated in live trees, 1-5 metres above ground. 4-6 eggs.

Nesting Location

Northern Flicker
Colaptes auratus

Size Identification

Foot: Zygodactyl

Egg: Actual Size

Backyard Feeder

Observation Calendar

J F M A M J J A S O N D

Male: Grey at top of head which stops at bright red spot on back of neck; black eye is encircled in light brown, with a black line running off bill to lower neck; chest begins with black half-moon necklace on front and turns into a white belly with black spots; wings and tail greyish-brown with black banding; white rump; yellow feathers are evident under sharp pointed tail feathers while in flight.

Female: Similar to male except without the black line running from bill.

Voice: Various sounds depending on its use. When claiming its territory a series of *kekekekeke* and when in courtship *woeka-woeka-woeka*.

Food: Digs and pokes on the ground looking for ants and other insects, fruit and seeds. Most of its diet consists of ants.

Nest/Eggs: Cavity of tree with no added material, .5-18 metres above ground. 3-10 eggs.

Nesting Location

Pileated Woodpecker
Dryocopus pileatus

Size Identification

Foot: Zygodactyl

Egg: Actual Size

Backyard Feeder

Observation Calendar

J F M A M J J A S O N D

Male: Crow-sized woodpecker with a distinctive red crest at top; red band running from black bill to cheek; black extends down neck to tail; cheeks and throat have white banding. *In flight:* White patches are visible on wings; feet and legs black.
Female: Black forehead replaces portion of red crest. No red band from bill to cheek.

Did you know? The Pileated Woodpecker can be so aggressive when chiseling away at trees that it can weaken the tree to falling point.

Voice: A quick set of calls, *whucker whucker whucker* in duets, sometimes followed by a sharp *kuk* when contacting mate.
Food: Larvae, ants and tree-dwelling insects, wild fruits, acorns, beechnuts.
Nest/Eggs: Cavity of tree with no added material. 3-4 eggs.

Nesting Location

Olive-sided Flycatcher

Contopus cooperi

Observation Calendar

J F M A M J J A S O N D

Male/Female: Dark grey/olive overall with crest at back of head; bar of white that runs down front from under chin to lower belly; white tufts on sides of rump but could be hidden by wings; feet and legs black; bill black on top with yellow underside.

Voice: A loud whistled hick, *three-bee-er* with first word quieter than others and the second accented. A warning *chirp pip pip pip.*
Food: Flying insects.
Nest/Eggs: Flat cup attached to horizontal branch of conifer tree or shrub built with twigs, small roots and lichens and lined with pine needles and small roots, 2-15 metres above ground. 3 eggs.

Eastern Wood-Pewee
Contopus virens

Foot: Anisodactyl

Egg: Actual Size

Observation Calendar
J F M A M J J A S O N D

Male/Female: Olive-grey overall with head that is crested at back; wings black and dark grey with two white bars; throat and chest white; belly slightly yellow or white; tail charcoal; bill black on top and yellow underside; feet and legs black.

Did you know? The Wood-Pewee changes its voice in morning and evening, converting its song into a slow verse.

Voice: A soft whistle *pee-a-wee pee-awee* repeated without any pause early in the morning.
Food: Flies, beetles, bees, ants and other insects.
Nest/Eggs: Shallow cup built with grass, spider's web and fibres, lined with hair, covered outside with lichens, on horizontal branch of tree far out from trunk, 5-20 metres above ground. 3-5 eggs.

Nesting Location

Yellow-bellied Flycatcher

Empidonax flaviventris

Foot: Anisodactyl

Observation Calendar

J F M A M J J A S O N D

Male: Olive-green head, back, wings and tail feathers; yellowish throat and breast; wings have two yellow bands; black eye has yellow ring; feet and legs black; thin bill is dark grey on top with yellow underside or it can be all dark.

Voice: A simple and sweet *pu-wee peawee.*
Food: Flying insects.
Nest/Eggs: Deep cup built with mosses and lined with black rootlets, pine needles, grass and moss, on or near ground, at base of conifer tree. 3-4 eggs.

Nesting Location

Willow Flycatcher

Empidonax traillii

Size Identification

Foot: Anisodactyl

Egg: Actual Size

Observation Calendar
J F M A M J J A S O N D

Male/Female: Olive-brown upperparts; white throat; chest and belly tinted yellow; feet and legs black; two rows of white banding on wings; faint eye ring.

Food: Flying insects.
Voice: Song is accented on the first note. Song is *Fitsbyou*. Call is *wit*.
Nest/Eggs: Cup-shaped nest built from and lined with plant fibres. 3-4 eggs.

Nesting Location

148

Least Flycatcher

Empidonax minimus

Size Identification

Foot: Anisodactyl

Observation Calendar

J F M A M J J A S O N D

Male/Female: Smallest of the flycatchers with a brown/olive head and back; rump is slightly golden; throat white and washes to a grey breast and a pale yellow belly; black eye is ringed with white; wings dark brown and black with white wing bands; tail dark olive/brown with white edges.

Did you know? The Least Flycatcher is not afraid of humans and in pursuit of a flying insect will dive within inches of a person.

Voice: Song is *chibic chibic chibic* repeated with accent in middle of phrase.

Food: Flying insects.

Nest/Eggs: Compact and deep cup built with bark, weeds, grasses and lined with thistle, feathers, hair and fibres, in upright fork of tree or shrub, 1-20 metres above ground. 3-6 eggs.

Egg: Actual Size

Nesting Location

Eastern Phoebe

Sayornis phoebe

Size Identification

Foot: Anisodactyl

Egg: Actual Size

Observation Calendar

J F M A M J J A S O N D

Male/Female: Grey-brown head and back with white throat, chest and belly; feet and legs black; white wing bands; pale yellow belly.

Did you know? One quick way to identify this bird is to watch the greyish brown tail bobbing up and down.

Voice: Song is rough sounding *fee bee fee bee*. Call is *wit*.
Food: Flying insects as well as ground insects.
Nest/Eggs: Large shelf structure built with weeds, grass, fibres and mud, covered with moss, lined with grass and hair. 3-6 eggs. Often nests in building eavestroughing.

Nesting Location

Great Crested Flycatcher

Myiarchus crinitus

Foot: Anisodactyl

Observation Calendar

J F M A M J J A S O N D

Egg: Actual Size

Male/Female: Olive/grey head with crest; back is olive/grey; wings are black with olive/grey edges and rust colour on outer edge; tail strong reddish-brown; throat soft grey changing to pale yellow at belly; feet and legs black.

Did you know? The Great Crested Flycatcher will sometimes use foil or cellophane in its nest because it is attracted to reflective objects.

Voice: A throaty whistle *wheeep* or a rolling *prrrreeeet*.
Food: Flying insects and a variety of ground insects.
Nest/Eggs: Bulky cup built with twig, leaves, feather, bark and cast off snakeskin, or Cellophane, in natural cavity of tree, up to 18 metres above ground. 4-8 eggs.

Birdhouse Nester

Nesting Location

Eastern Kingbird
Tyrannus tyrannus

Size Identification

Foot: Anisodactyl

Egg: Actual Size

Observation Calendar

J F M A M J J A S O N D

Male/Female: Black head, back, wings and tail; white chin, chest and belly; wings have white along edge and tail has white band along tip; feet and legs black.

Did you know? Size does not matter to the Eastern Kingbird: it will attack crows, ravens, hawks and owls to defend its territory.

Voice: Several different calls including *tzi tzee* as a true song. Also a *kitter kitter kitter* when threatened.
Food: Flying insects and fruit in late summer.
Nest/Eggs: Bulky cup built with weed stalks, grass and moss, in branches of tree or shrub, 3-6 metres above ground. 3-5 eggs.

Nesting Location

Loggerhead Shrike

Lanius ludovicianus

Size Identification

Foot: Anisodactyl

Egg: Actual Size

Male/Female: Grey overall body; distinct black mask; short black bill slightly curved at tip; chin, chest and belly grey; tail feathers black with white edges; feet and legs black.

Did you know? The Loggerhead Shrike stores freshly caught food by impaling it on thorns.

Voice: Call is *chak chak* along with a series of whistles.
Food: Small mammals, insects, small birds.
Nest/Eggs: Cuplike nest built of twigs and mosses, in tree or bush. 4-6 eggs.

Nesting Location

Northern Shrike
Lunius excubitor

Size Identification

Foot: Anisodactyl

Observation Calendar

J F M A M J J A S O N D

Male/Female: Black mask that may be dull at times; long sharp hooked black bill; head and back grey; throat, chest and belly soft grey with light grey banding from chest to lower belly; feet and legs black; wings and tail black with white edges.

Did you know? This bird is more like a hawk or owl because of its diet and hunting technique. Once the Northern Shrike has caught its prey it will often hang it in a thorny bush, saving it for later.

Voice: A light song *queeedle queeedle* along with *tsurp-see tsurpsee.*
Food: Small birds and mammals, but diet consists mainly of grasshoppers, locust, crickets and other large insects.
Nest/Eggs: Bulky woven cup built with sticks, twigs, grass and small roots, lined with cotton, feather and bark, in tree or shrub, up to 10 metres above ground. 4-7 eggs.

Nesting Location

Blue-headed Vireo

Vireo solitarius

Foot: Anisodactyl

Observation Calendar

J F M A M J J A S O N D

Male/Female: Blue-grey head and back with shades of olive along back; eye is brown with distinctive white eyebrow encircling it; bill long and black; feet and legs charcoal; throat and belly white with olive along edges of belly; tail charcoal with white edges.

Egg: Actual Size

Did you know? Although these birds are not common in parks, they are very tame when approached. Sometimes they will continue to sit on their nest even in the presence of humans, while other birds would probably attack or retreat from the area with a few choice tweeeeps.

Voice: The song is a series of short whistled phrases interrupted by pauses, similar to the Red-eyed Vireo but higher pitched and sweeter.
Food: Small insects, fruit.
Nest/Eggs: Suspended basketlike cup built with bark, fibre, grass, small roots and hair in a tree, 1-6 metres above ground. 3-5 eggs.

Nesting Location

Warbling Vireo

Vireo gilvus

Size Identification

Foot: Anisodactyl

Egg: Actual Size

Observation Calendar

J F M A M J J A S O N D

Male/Female: Grey and green head, neck and back; white eyebrow extending from black bill; white chin, breast and belly with variable amounts of yellow; feet and legs black; tail and wings black with white edging.

Voice: The best way to find a Warbling Vireo is to listen. This bird sings throughout the day with a beautiful warbling sound. Song is a group of slurred phrases such as *brig-a-dier brig-a-dier brigate.*
Food: Small insects including caterpillars, beetles and moths, some berries.
Nest/Eggs: Tightly woven pensile cup built with bark, leaves, grass, feathers, plant down and spider's web, lined with stems and horsehair, suspended in tall trees at the edge of wooded area, well away from trunk. 3-5 eggs.

Nesting Location

Red-eyed Vireo

Vireo olivaceus

Foot: Anisodactyl

J F M A M J J A S O N D

Egg: Actual Size

Male/Female: *Spring:* red eye encircled with thin line of black set against a wide white eyebrow that runs from bill to back of head; black bill; throat and chest white; feet and legs black; back and rump are olive green; wings and tail black with edges of olive green; eye is darker brown in winter.

Voice: The Red-eyed Vireo may sound over 40 different phrases in just 60 seconds, then begin all over again. A variety of short phrases, which include *cherrrwit chereeee cissy a witt teeeooo.*
Food: Small insects, berries, fruit.
Nest/Eggs: Deep cup built with grass, paper, bark, rootlets, vine and decorated outside with spider's web and lichen, suspended in branches, .5-18 metres above ground. 2 eggs.

Nesting Location

Blue Jay

Cyanocitta cristata

Size Identification

Foot: Anisodactyl

Egg: Actual Size

Backyard Feeder

Observation Calendar

J F M A M J J A S O N D

Male/Female: Bright blue crested head with black band running through eye to just under crest on back of neck; black band continues along side of neck on both sides to chest; white under chin; back is blue; wings and tail are blue banded with black and tipped with white at ends; black bill is large with light feathers covering nostril area; feet and legs black.

Did you know? The Blue Jay has a bad reputation for eating eggs of other birds, and even their young.

Voice: Call is *jay jay jay*, plus many other calls including mimicking hawks.

Food: Omnivorous — in summer months the Blue Jay feasts on just about anything, including spiders, snails, salamanders, frogs, seeds and caterpillars. In winter months it supplements its diet with acorns and other nuts stored in tree cavities earlier in the year.

Nest/Eggs: Bulky nest of sticks, leaves, string and moss, lined with small roots, well hidden, 1-15 metres above ground, in tree or shrub. 3-4 eggs.

Nesting Location

158

American Crow

Corvus brachyrhynchos

Foot: Anisodactyl

Observation Calendar

J F M A M J J A S O N D

Male/Female: Overall shiny black with a hint of purple in direct sunlight; large broad black bill; short and slightly square tail; feet and legs black.

Egg: Actual Size

Did you know? Although one might think that crows are a nuisance, they actually devour large quantities of grasshoppers, beetles and grubs that can be destructive to crops.

Voice: A variety of calls. Most common is the long *caaaaaw* which softens at the end.

Food: Omnivorous — insects, food waste, grains, seeds and carrion.

Nest/Eggs: Large basket of twigs, sticks, vines, moss, feathers, fur and hair, on ledge in crotch of tree or shrub. 3-4 eggs.

Backyard Feeder

Nesting Location

Common Raven

Corvus corax

Observation Calendar

J F M A M J J A S O N D

Male/Female: Shiny, black bird overall with a blue tint; feet and legs black; black bill is long and wide and has been described as a "Roman nose"; rounded tail.

Voice: Variety of calls including buzzing, croaks and gulps.
Food: A variety of insects, carrion, small mammals and food waste.
Nest/Eggs: Large basket of twigs, sticks, vines, hair and moss, lined with animal hair, on ledge, in tree or shrub. 3-4 eggs.

Horned Lark

Eremophila alpestris

Foot: Anisodactyl

Observation Calendar
J F M A M J J A S O N D

Male/Female: Dull brown on top; chest and belly white; wings and tail brown and black; distinctive black facial marks which include small horns (feathers) on either side of its head; chin pale yellow with black band above running through eye and down; feet and legs black.

Egg: Actual Size

Did you know? The horns are not always visible, but a quick way to identify the Horned Lark is that on the ground it walks and does not hop, like most small birds.

Voice: Soft twittering *tsee titi* or *zzeeet*.
Food: A variety of insects, seeds and grains.
Nest/Eggs: Hollow in ground under grass tuft, made of stems and leaves, lined with grass. 3-5 eggs.

Nesting Location

Purple Martin

Progne subis

Size Identification

Feet: Anisodactyl

Egg: Actual Size

Observation Calendar

J F M A M J J A S O N D

Male: Very shiny, dark purple overall, with black wings and tail; black bill is short and slightly curved; feet and legs reddish, black; wings very long reaching to tip of tail when folded.
Female: Dull purple head and back with black wings and tail; chest and chin grey; belly white with black speckles; feet and legs black.

Voice: Call is high pitched *cheer cheer.*
Food: Flying insects.
Nest/Eggs: Deep cup in cavity lined with grass and leaves, usually in large colonies. Nests in gourds and special martin houses. 3-8 eggs.

Birdhouse Nester

Nesting Location

Tree Swallow

Tachycineta bicolor

Size Identification

Foot: Anisodactyl

Observation Calendar

J F M A M J J A S O N D

Egg: Actual Size

Male/Female: Dark iridescent blue on head, neck, back, wings and tail; bright white chin, chest and belly; black bill is short and slightly curved; wings are very long, reaching down to tip of tail when folded; feet and legs charcoal.

Did you know? The Tree Swallow is the only swallow that eats berries in the place of insects. This allows it to winter further north than its relatives.

Voice: Early morning song *wheet trit weet*, with an alarm call of *cheedeeep*.
Food: Flying insects, berries.
Nest/Eggs: Cup in cavity of tree lined with grass and feathers, usually a woodpecker's old hole. 4-6 eggs.

Birdhouse Nester

Nesting Location

Northern Rough-winged Swallow

Stelgidopteryx serripennis

Size Identification

Foot: Anisodactyl

Egg: Actual Size

Observation Calendar
J F M A M J J A S O N D

Male/Female: Greyish pale brown upper parts; pale brown chin, chest and sides; white belly; feet and legs black; short black beak; short tail.

Voice: Harsh *brrrrrt* during aggression or danger. Musical *br rrrrt* drawn out and often doubled.
Food: Insects in flight.
Nest/Eggs: Built in cavities such as tunnels, bridges, culverts and caves, lined with grass, leaves and moss. Often with swallows in crevices in cliff faces. 4-8 eggs.

Nesting Location

164

Bank Swallow

Riparia riparia

Size Identification

Foot: Anisodactyl

Observation Calendar

J F M A M J J A S O N D

Male/Female: Dirty brown overall with white front except for brown band running across chest; wings are very long, reaching down to tip of tail when folded; feet and legs grey; black bill is short and curved.

Voice: A variety of calls including *tchirrt tchirrt* and long twittering.

Food: Flying insects as well as a variety of other insects. Main diet consists of dragonflies, flies, mayflies and beetles.

Nest/Eggs: Earth tunnel lined with grass and straw, along bank of water. 4-6 eggs.

Egg: Actual Size

Nesting Location

Cliff Swallow
Petrochelidon pyrrhonota

Size Identification

Foot: Anisodactyl

Egg: Actual Size

Observation Calendar
J F M A M J J A S O N D

Male/Female: Overall black with buff rump and brick red cheeks; white patch on forehead; belly white; back has variable amounts of white streaks; feet and legs grey; tail black, square at end.

Did you know? Nest sights can be a little competitive and the birds will steal nesting grasses and twigs from each other's nests.

Voice: A long *chuuurrrr* and a deeper *nyeeew*.
Food: A variety of insects.
Nest/Eggs: Mud lined with grass, hair and feathers, under bridges, in cliffs and buildings. 3-6 eggs.

Nesting Location

Barn Swallow

Hirundo rustica

Size Identification

Foot: Anisodactyl

Observation Calendar

J F M A M J J A S O N D

Male: Dark blue iridescent from top of head, shoulders, down back and top of wings; chin and chest rust colour that fades to white at belly; wings are very long and extend to tips of tail, which is forked with long feathers at either end that can be seen when bird is in flight; feet and legs charcoal; black and cream bill. When bird is in flight a band of white can be seen at end of wings.
Female: Same markings but duller.

Egg: Actual Size

Did you know? Barn Swallows are amazing to watch as they skim over water and pick insects off the surface. In the evening they hunt mosquitoes.

Voice: A soft twittering *kvik kvik wit wit.*
Food: A variety of insects.
Nest/Eggs: Mud and straw, lined with feathers, in buildings, under bridges, in cliffs and caves. 4-5 eggs.

Nesting Location

Black-capped Chickadee

Poecile atricapilla

Size Identification

Foot: Anisodactyl

Egg: Actual Size

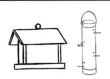

Backyard Feeder

Birdhouse Nester

Nesting Location

Observation Calendar

J F M A M J J A S O N D

Male/Female: Round black head with white cheeks; black chin that contrasts against bright white bib which fades into rust on belly with buff edges; wings black and grey with white edges; tail black with white edges; feet and legs black.

Did you know? In winter Black-capped Chickadees form small flocks of about 10 birds and defend their territory from intruders.

Voice: A descending whistle with two notes and sounds like *chick-a-dee-dee-dee.*
Food: Seeds, insects, berries. Drawn to thistle-seed feeders.
Nest/Eggs: Domed cup lined with wool, hair, fur, moss and insect cocoons, in cavity of tree. 5-10 eggs.

Red-breasted Nuthatch

Sitta canadensis

Foot: Anisodactyl

Observation Calendar

J F M A M J J A S O N D

Male: Small round bird with black stripe over top of head and white stripe underneath running over eye to back of head, followed by another black band running through eye; white cheeks turn to rust at neck and continue rust to chest and belly; back is grey-blue; wings and tail grey becoming black at ends; black bill is often white on underside; feet and legs brown-black.
Female: Similar to male except for grey cap and light underside.

Did you know? The Red-breasted Nuthatch will smear pitch at the entrance to its nest, although it is not known why.

Voice: A tin-whistle call and an occasional loud *knack knack*.
Food: Seeds, insects, flying insects.
Nest/Eggs: Cup lined with grass, moss and feathers, in excavated cavity or crevice of tree, 1-12 metres above ground. 4-7 eggs.

Egg: Actual Size

Backyard Feeder

Birdhouse Nester

Nesting Location

White-breasted Nuthatch

Sitta carolinensis

Size Identification

Foot: Anisodactyl

Egg: Actual Size

Observation Calendar
J F M A M J J A S O N D

Male: Shiny black on top of head running down the back, turning to lighter blue-grey on back; face and neck white, which runs down chest and belly; slight rust colours on sides; wings and tail are blue-grey with white edges; feet and legs black.
Female: Similar to male except top of head and back are lighter grey.

Did you know? These little birds are known for their ability to run down tree trunks headfirst, at a very fast pace.

Backyard Feeder

Voice: Nesting pairs keep in contact with one another with a deep sounding *aank aank* but also chatter a soft *ip ip*.
Food: Spiders, insects, seeds, insect eggs, acorns.
Nest/Eggs: Cup lined with twigs, feathers, small roots, fur and hair, in natural cavity or crevice of tree, 4-15 metres above ground. 5-10 eggs.

Birdhouse Nester

Nesting Location

170

Brown Creeper
Certhia americana

Size Identification

Foot: Anisodactyl

Observation Calendar
J F M A M J J A S O N D

Male/Female: Overall brown with grey streaks and white chin, chest and belly; long curved bill that is black on top and white/pink on bottom; distinctive eye stripe; feet and legs grey; tail is long and pointed.

Did you know? Spending most of its day creeping up and down trees looking for meals, the Brown Creeper can flatten itself and blend into the colour of the tree trunk when a predator passes by.

Backyard Feeder

Voice: A very high whistling *see wee see tu eee*.
Food: Insects, insect and spider eggs and occasionally nuts and seeds.
Nest/Eggs: Cup with foundation of twigs, bark, and leaves, lined with bark, grass, feathers and moss, in cavity or under loose bark of tree, up to 5 metres above ground. 4-8 eggs.

Birdhouse Nester

Nesting Location

Carolina Wren

Thryothorus ludovicianus

Size Identification

Foot: Anisodactyl

Egg: Actual Size

Observation Calendar

J F M A M J J A S O N D

Male/Female: Overall brown body with warmer brown on upperparts; distinct white eyebrow; long tail with black banding; feet and legs brown; white rump.

Did you know? The Carolina Wren usually holds its tail cocked upright.

Voice: Variety of notes and trills. Song is *tea kettle, tea kettle*. Call is *chip*.
Food: Insects, spiders.
Nest/Eggs: Cavity nest built with hair, twigs and grasses and lined with feathers and soft grasses. 4-6 eggs.

Birdhouse Nester

Nesting Location

House Wren

Troglodytes aedon

Size Identification

Foot: Anisodactyl

Observation Calendar

J F M A M J J A S O N D

Egg: Actual Size

Male/Female: Brown upper parts; light buff eyebrows; short rust and black-banded tail that is often cocked; light buff chin, chest and belly; light buff banding along sides; feet and legs greyish-pink; sharp black beak with yellow lower mandible.

Voice: Warbling that descends for 2-3 seconds. Call is a variety of buzzes and rattling *chur*.
Food: Insects.
Nest/Eggs: In cavities of trees or birdhouses, twigs lined with softer material including moss, feathers, rootlets and grasses. 5-6 eggs.

Birdhouse Nester

Nesting Location

Winter Wren

Troglodytes troglodytes

Size Identification

Foot: Anisodactyl

Egg: Actual Size

Observation Calendar

J F M A M J J A S O N D

Male/Female: One of the smallest wrens, with a very short tail; mixed browns on head and back with faint banding in black; wings and tail brown with black banding; feet and legs red; black bill is slightly white on underside; long talons.

Did you know? You may think you are seeing a mouse when you first spot the Winter Wren. It likes to keep near the ground and its movements are similar to a field mouse.

Voice: Call is *chip chip* with a variety of songs including twittering and twinkles.
Food: Insects, insect eggs, spiders.
Nest/Eggs: Domed cup under roots in tangled growth near ground built with weed, twig, moss, grass and lined with hair and feather. 4-7 eggs.

Nesting Location

Marsh Wren
Cistothorus palustris

Foot: Anisodactyl

J F M A M J J A S O N D

Male/Female: Overall reddish-brown; white streaks on head and back; extremely dark brown crown; white eyebrow; white throat and chest; feet and legs red.

Egg: Actual Size

Did you know? The male will build a number of different courting nests during mating season and will sometimes take several different mates during the same season.

Voice: Song is a low rattling mechanical trill. Call is *chek* repeated.
Food: Insects. Occasionally small bird eggs.
Nest/Eggs: Ball-shaped nest built with wet reeds, grasses and cattails then lined with plant and feather down, 1-3 feet above ground and secured to aquatic plants. 3-8 eggs.

Nesting Location

Golden-crowned Kinglet

Regulus satrapa

Observation Calendar

J F M A M J J A S O N D

Male: One of the smallest woodland birds, with black head stripes that set off its crown patch of orange with yellow edges; neck and back olive-grey; wings and tail black with olive along edges; feet and legs black; pale grey wingbars; pale eyebrow.

Female: Similar to male except patch on top is yellow.

Did you know? Their movements on a tree make them easy to spot. They flutter their wings as they look for insects.

Voice: Very high-pitched, dropping to a quick chatter. The song is so highly pitched that some people cannot hear it.

Food: A variety of insects, spiders, fruits and seeds.

Nest/Eggs: Deep cup built with moss and lichen at top, lined with black rootlets and feathers suspended from conifer branch, up to 30 metres above ground. 5-11 eggs.

Ruby-crowned Kinglet

Regulus calendula

Observation Calendar
J F M A M J J A S O N D

Male: Olive-grey overall with white eye ring broken at top; crested with red patch on head; chin and neck are lighter olive-grey; feet and legs black; wings and tail black with white edges; white bands on wings.

Female: Similar to male except for no red patch on top of head.

Did you know? The ruby red top on the male is hard to see except when he is courting when, it will flare up.

Voice: High pitched *tee tee tee* followed by a lower *tew tew tew* and ending with a chatter.

Food: Insects, insect eggs, spiders, fruits, seeds.

Nest/Eggs: Deep woven cup built with moss, lichen at top and lined with small black roots and feathers, suspended from conifer branch. 5-10 eggs.

Blue-gray Gnatcatcher
Polioptila caerulea

Size Identification

Egg: Actual Size

Observation Calendar
J F M A M J J A S O N D

Male: Overall dark bluish-grey upperparts; white chin, chest and belly; long black tail with white below; white eye ring; sharp black bill; black feet and legs; black eyebrow during mating season.
Female: No black eyebrow during mating season.

Did you know? The Blue-gray Gnatcatcher was named for its feeding behaviour. The bird will dart out from trees and catch gnats and flies in midair.

Voice: Song is a buzzing sound like that a grasshopper makes. Call is *zeeeeee*.
Food: Flying insects, larvae, spiders.
Nest/Eggs: Cup built with spider silk, plant fibres and down then lined with finer materials such as lichen and moss, 0.6-24 metres above ground in fork of tree. 3-6 eggs.

Nesting Location

Eastern Bluebird

Sialia sialis

Size Identification

Foot: Anisodactyl

J F M A M J J A S O N D

Male: Bright blue upper parts; tan throat and sides; white belly; feet and legs black.
Female: Similar to male except paler and head has greyish spotting.

Voice: Song is bright whistle *cheer cheerful charmer*. Call is lower *turrweee*.
Food: Variety of insects. Visits feeders for peanut butter, berries, mealworm or raisins.
Nest/Eggs: Built in cavity of tree or birdhouse from a variety of grasses and pine needles, lined with softer material. 3-6 eggs.

Egg: Actual Size

Backyard Feeder

Birdhouse Nester

Nesting Location

179

Veery
Catharus fuscescens

Size Identification

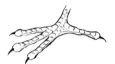

Foot: Anisodactyl

Egg: Actual Size

Observation Calendar

J F M A M J J A S O N D

Male/Female: Overall reddish-brown upper parts; white buff chest and belly; soft tan spotting along chin and cheeks; grey sides; feet and legs pinkish-grey.

Voice: Soft descending notes — *turreeooreooo-reeoorreeo*. Call is a loud descending *veerr*.
Food: Various insects, larvae, snails, earthworms, spiders and wild berries.
Nest/Eggs: Built of stems, twigs and mosses, lined with softer material including various grasses and rootlets. 3-5 eggs.

Nesting Location

Gray-cheeked Thrush
Catharus minimus

Size Identification

Foot: Anisodactyl

Observation Calendar
J F M A M J J A S O N D

Male/Female: Overall dusty greyish-brown; white neck, chest and belly with bold spotting; faint eye ring; feet and legs pinkish.

Voice: Song is a descending whistle. Call is a descending *weeeoooh*.
Food: Insects, spiders, crayfish, berries, earthworms, caterpillars.

Nesting Location

Swainson's Thrush
Catharus ustululus

Size Identification

Foot: Anisodactyl

Egg: Actual Size

Observation Calendar

J F M A M J J A S O N D

Male/Female: Overall-greyish brown with white belly and throat, which has dark banding; buff eye ring; pink-grey feet and legs.

Did you know? Very vocal bird during feeding. Swainson's Thrush is often seen with large flocks of other birds including warblers.

Voice: Series of rising whistling voice. Short call *whit* and *peeep*.
Food: Insects, fruits, spiders.
Nest/Eggs: Cuplike consisting of grasses, plant fibres and lichens, 1-5 metres above ground. 3-5 eggs.

Nesting Location

Hermit Thrush

Catharus guttatus

Foot: Anisodactyl

Observation Calendar

J F M A M J J A S O N D

Male/Female: Dusty brown head, neck and back that blends into a rust tail; white eye ring; wings rust when open with black ends; neck and chest white and dark spotted; underparts grey; feet and legs grey with pink; bill black and rust.

Egg: Actual Size

Did you know? Not surprisingly, a Hermit Thrush prefers the seclusion of deep wooded areas.

Voice: Sweet song with a variety of phrases. When disturbed it sounds a *kuk kuk kuk kuk*.
Food: A variety of insects, worms, caterpillars, snails and various fruits.
Nest/Eggs: Bulky ground nest built with twigs, bark, grass and moss and lined with conifer needles, fibre and small roots, in damp and cool wooded areas. 3-4 eggs.

Nesting Location

Wood Thrush

Hylocichla mustelina

Size Identification

Foot: Anisodactyl

Egg: Actual Size

Observation Calendar

J F M A M J J A S O N D

Male/Female: Rust coloured head fades to a brown back; wings and tail dark brown with black ends; feet and legs grey with pink; black bill has light yellow on underside; white eye ring; chin and chest white with black spotting; underparts grey.

Voice: Suggestive of flute, the song is a series of varied phrases *ee oh lee ee oh lay*.
Food: A variety of insects on the ground and in trees.
Nest/Eggs: Firm and compact cup built with grass, paper, moss, bark and mud, lined with small roots in tree or shrub, 2-15 metres above ground. 3-4 eggs.

Nesting Location

American Robin
Turdus migratorius

Size Identification

Foot: Anisodactyl

Observation Calendar
J F M A M J J A S O N D

Male: Charcoal/brown head with distinctive white above and below eye; back and wings charcoal brown with white edges; tail dark grey; neck dark grey with thin white banding; chest and belly brick red; feet and legs black; bill yellow with black at either end.
Female: Breast is slightly paler than male's.

Voice: Song is *cheerily cheerily cheerily* in a whistle tone.
Food: Earthworms, insects, fruit.
Nest/Eggs: Deep cup built with weed stalks, cloth, string and mud, lined with grass, in evergreens and deciduous trees or shrubs. 4 eggs.

Egg: Actual Size

Backyard Feeder

Nesting Location

Gray Catbird

Dumetella carolinensis

Size Identification

Foot: Anisodactyl

Egg: Actual Size

Observation Calendar

J F M A M J J A S O N D

Male/Female: Distinctive black cap with overall grey body; brick red rump which is hidden most of the time; feet and legs grey with hints of pink.

Did you know? Catbirds actually migrate during the night hours and research indicates they use the moon for navigating.

Voice: A distinctive catlike song: *meeow* and *kwut.*
Food: A variety of insects, spiders and wild berries.
Nest/Eggs: Bulky deep cup built with twigs, vines, grass, paper and weeds, lined with small roots, in dense thickets of tree or shrub, 1-3 metres above ground. 3-6 eggs.

Nesting Location

Northern Mockingbird

Mimus polyglottos

Size Identification

Foot: Anisodactyl

Observation Calendar
J F M A M J J A S O N D

Male/Female: Grey overall upperparts; white chin, chest and belly; tail long with white edging; reddish-brown eye; feet and legs black. *In flight*: Small white patch on inner part of primaries.

Egg: Actual Size

Did you know? The mocking bird gets its name from its habit of mimicking other bird songs, usually repeating them several times.

Voice: Song mimics other song birds. Call is loud *chewk*.
Food: Insects, spiders, snakes and various other reptiles, fruits, berries.
Nest/Eggs: Built of twigs, grasses, dry leaves and various found objects such as cloth, well concealed within a shrub. 2-6 eggs.

Backyard Feeder

Nesting Location

Brown Thrasher
Toxostoma rufum

Size Identification

Foot: Anisodactyl

Egg: Actual Size

Observation Calendar

J F M A M J J A S O N D

Male/Female: Distinctive long black bill; grey chin; white chest and belly streaked with dark brown; long reddish-brown tail and back; reddish-brown crown on head; feet and legs pinkish-grey; white and black banding on wings.

Voice: Call is a loud *smack*. Voice mimics other birds and is usually repeated twice.
Food: Variety of insects, frogs, lizards, snakes and various wild berries.
Nest/Eggs: Built of twigs, sticks and dead leaves, lined with softer material including grasses and rootlets. 2-6 eggs.

Nesting Location

European Starling
Sturnus vulgaris

Foot: Anisodactyl

Egg: Actual Size

Backyard Feeder

Birdhouse Nester

Nesting Location

Observation Calendar
J F M A M J J A S O N D

Male/Female: *Summer*: Black iridescent bird in summer with light white speckles over entire body; bill is sharp yellow; wing and tail are edged in white and brown; feet and legs are red. *Winter*: Speckles increase and some become brown; bill is black; feet and legs are red; wings and tail have more brown.

Did you know? Sixty starlings were introduced into New York City in 1890. Since then they have spread throughout North America.

Voice: Mimics the songs of other birds and even the sounds of cats and whistles.
Food: A variety of insects, worms, grubs and weed seeds.
Nest/Eggs: Loose cup in cavity filled with grass, leaves, cloth and feathers, up to 18 metres above the ground. 4-5 eggs.

American Pipit
Anthus rubescens

Size Identification

Foot: Anisodactyl

Observation Calendar
J F M A M J J A S O N D

Male/Female: *Summer*: Grey-brown on upperparts; light buff breast and belly; chest streaked with brown; buff eyebrow; dark cheek; feet and legs dark brown or black; short brown tail bobs while feeding. *Winter*: Similar to summer except brown upperparts; breast heavily streaked with dark brown.

Voice: Song is repeated *chiweee*. Call is short *peet peet*.
Food: Insects, seeds, weeds, crustaceans, molluscs.

Nesting Location

Cedar Waxwing

Bombycilla cedrorum

Foot: Anisodactyl

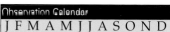

Observation Calendar

J F M A M J J A S O N D

Egg: Actual Size

Male/Female: Crested brown head with black mask running from black bill, through eyes, to behind head; white outline around mask; back brown; chest and belly yellow-brown; wings black-grey with white edges; wings and tail have red tips; rump white.

Did you know? The name derives from the fact that the wings and tail look as though they have been dipped in red wax.

Voice: Extremely high-pitched *seeee*.
Food: A variety of berries.
Nest/Eggs: Loose woven cup of grass, twigs, cotton fibre and string, lined with small roots, fine grass and down, in open wooded areas in tree or shrub, 2-6 metres above ground. 4-5 eggs.

Nesting Location

Blue-winged Warbler

Vermivora pinus

Observation Calendar

J F M A M J J A S O N D

Male/Female: Yellow overall; grey wings; sharp black bill; black line through eye; tail light grey; white undertail coverts; grey feet and legs.

Voice: *Beeee buzzzz* sounding note.
Food: Insects, spiders.
Nest/Eggs: Cone-shaped nest built with grasses, bark and leaves, on or near ground. 5 eggs.

Golden-winged Warbler

Vermivora chrysoptera

Foot: Anisodactyl

Observation Calendar

J F M A M J J A S O N D

Male/Female: Grey overall with bright yellow wing patch; yellow cap; black mask on face with white banding on top and bottom reaching to cheek; feet and legs black.

Egg: Actual Size

Voice: Song is buzzing *zeee beee beee*. Call is single *chip*.
Food: Insects, spiders.
Nest/Eggs: Cup-shaped nest built of grasses, leaves and grapevine, hidden on ground. 3-6 eggs.

Nesting Location

193

Tennessee Warbler

Vermivora peregrina

Observation Calendar

J F M A M J J A S O N D

Male: Grey upperparts with greenish back; white eyebrow; slightly curved black bill; black feet and legs; green rump with white underparts.
Female: Similar but olive-green overall.

Voice: Loud repeated notes *tsit tsit tsit tsut tsut*, *tee tee tee*. Call is *chirp*.
Food: Fruit, insects, spiders.

Orange-crowned Warbler

Vermivora celata

Foot: Anisodactyl

Observation Calendar

J F M A M J J A S O N D

Male/Female: Dull olive-green overall; pale olive-yellow underside; faint yellow streaks on side of chest; dark grey feet and legs; orange crown not visible.

Voice: Song is high-pitched trill. Call is *chet*.
Food: Insects, berries.

Nesting Location

Nashville Warbler

Vermivora ruficapilla

Size Identification

Foot: Anisodactyl

Egg: Actual Size

Observation Calendar

J F M A M J J A S O N D

Male/Female: Thin, very pointed bill; head and neck bluish-grey; eye ring white; upper parts olive-green; underparts yellow, white on belly.

Voice: Calls include *see it see it see it*, and *ti ti ti ti ti*.
Food: A variety of insects.
Nest/Eggs: Nest of moss or bark, lined with grass and hair, on ground. 4-5 eggs.

Nesting Location

Yellow Warbler

Dendroica petechia

Size Identification

Foot: Anisodactyl

Observation Calendar

J F M A M J J A S O N D

Male: Yellow throat and chest; olive back; wings and tail black and olive with yellow highlights; chest barred with chestnut strips; bill and feet reddish-black.
Female: Similar to male only darker and lacks chestnut markings on front chest.

Voice: A sweet and rapid *tsee, tsee, tsee, tsee, titi-wee.*
Food: Insects with large quantities of caterpillars, beetles and moths. Young birds are fed earthworms as well.
Nest/Eggs: Cup of milkweed, hair, down and fine grasses, built in upright fork of tree or bush. 3-6 eggs.

Egg: Actual Size

Nesting Location

Chestnut-sided Warbler

Dendroica pensylvanica

Observation Calendar

J F M A M J J A S O N D

Male: Bright lemon-yellow crown with chestnut down sides of chest; black band running through eye from black bill; black and white banding on back with yellow tinting; wings and tail black with white edges; feet and legs black; chin and belly white.
Female: Similar to male except mask is duller and chestnut on sides is reduced.

Did you know? Audubon declared these birds as rare but, with the clearing of woodland, sightings have increased.

Voice: A territorial song—*sweet sweet sweet I so sweet.*
Food: A variety of insects including caterpillars, moths and beetles.
Nest/Eggs: Loose cup of stems, grass and plant down, lined with grass and hair, in briar tangles, hedges or shrubs, up to 2 metres above ground. 3-5 eggs.

Magnolia Warbler

Dendroica magnolia

Foot: Anisodactyl

Observation Calendar

J F M A M J J A S O N D

Male: Grey head with small eyebrow stripe of white above eye; black mask; yellow chin; chest and belly yellow with black banding; back grey with black banding; wings and tail grey with white edges; two white wing bars; white rump.
Female: Similar to male except banding on chest is narrower; face is grey without black mask and white eyebrow; white eye ring.

Egg: Actual Size

Voice: A short melodic song *weeta weeta weeta wee*.
Food: A variety of insects and spiders.
Nest/Eggs: Loosely built cup nest of grass, moss and weed stalks, lined with dark roots, in small conifers along the edge of wooded areas and in gardens. 3-5 eggs.

Nesting Location

Cape May Warbler

Dendroica tigrina

Observation Calendar

J F M A M J J A S O N D

Male: *Spring*: Mostly yellow head with chestnut-orange patch below eye; darker cap; brown and black wings; yellow underparts streaked black; white wing patch; short brown tail. *Fall*: Duller overall but white wing patches still present.
Female: *Spring*: Yellow patch under grey cheek; two narrow white wing bars; paler yellow underparts lightly streaked. *Fall*: Overall dull.

Did you know? The Cape May Warbler will hover at the tips of branches in search of insects.

Voice: High-pitched *seet seeet seeet seet*. Call is high note, *tseee*.
Food: Spruce budworm and other insects.

Black-throated Blue Warbler

Dendroica caerulescens

Size Identification

Foot: Anisodactyl

Observation Calendar

J F M A M J J A S O N D

Egg: Actual Size

Male: Blue-grey head and back; black face mask with black bill; chest white; wings and tail black with white edges; feet and legs black.

Female: Olive-brown head, back and wings with lighter tone on chin, chest and belly; black bill; thin buff eyebrows; feet and legs black; wings and tail olive-brown with white edges.

Voice: A husky song, "I am soo lazzzzy," and a call that is flat *tip*.

Food: A variety of insects, fruits and seeds taken mainly on ground or low-lying branches.

Nest/Eggs: Bulky cup of spider's web, dead wood, twigs, leaves and grass, lined with dark rootlets, in tree or shrub close to ground. 3-5 eggs.

Nesting Location

Yellow-rumped Warbler

Dendroica coronata

Egg: Actual Size

Observation Calendar

J F M A M J J A S O N D

Male/Female: *Spring*: Yellow rump and yellow patch on either side of chest; yellow crest set against grey head; black mask running from black bill; back grey with black banding; wings and tail black with white edges; two white wing bars; chin white; chest white with black band; feet and legs charcoal; white eyebrow. *Fall*: Similar but duller markers, no black mask, more brown and buff overall.

Did you know? This very abundant warbler was once called Myrtle Warbler and was thought to be two different species because of its change of plumage.

Voice: Song is light musical notes. Call is *cheeeck*.
Food: A variety of insects and fruit.
Nest/Eggs: Deep cup of twigs, bark, plant down and fibres, lined with hair, feathers and fine grass, in tree or shrub near trunk. 3-5 eggs.

Nesting Location

Black-throated Green Warbler

Dendroica virens

Observation Calendar

J F M A M J J A S O N D

Male: Olive head and back; yellow around eyes and on cheeks; black throat and chest changing to speckled black on white on belly and chest; black banding along sides of belly; wings and tail are black with white edging; two white wing bars; feet and legs brown-black; white rump.

Female: Yellow on throat with minimal black.

Voice: Song has a variety of accents, *zee zee zee zuu zee*, and sounds like "sleep sleep little one sleep."

Food: Variety of insects and fruit.

Nest/Eggs: Compact cup of fine bark, twigs, grass, lichens and spider's web, lined with hair, fur, feathers and small roots, in tree or shrub, 1-25 metres above ground. 3-5 eggs.

Blackburnian Warbler

Dendroica fusca

Observation Calendar

J F M A M J J A S O N D

Male: Bright orange-yellow chin, top of head and eyebrow set against black; black band running through eye; back black with white banding; wings and tail black with white edges; large white band on wing; feet and legs red and black; rump white.
Female: Similar to male except orange-yellow is paler; cheeks grey; belly grey.

Voice: Variable song is high-pitched and thin with a mixture of signal chirps and trills, *tsip tsip tsip titi tzeeeeee.*
Food: A variety of insects and berries.
Nest/Eggs: Cup nest built with plant down and spider's web, lined with hair, small roots and grass, in tree or shrub, 25 metres above ground. 4-5 eggs.

Pine Warbler

Dendroica pinus

Size Identification

Foot: Anisodactyl

Observation Calendar

J F M A M J J A S O N D

Male/Female: Olive-green upperparts; yellow chin, chest and belly; dark wings with two rows of white wing bands; feet and legs black.

Did you know? The Pine Warbler's name is derived from the fact that it is usually seen in pine trees and is fairly common in mature pine plantations.

Voice: Song is a trill in same key.
Food: Insects, spiders, fruit, berries.
Nest/Eggs: Cup-shaped nest built of twigs, bark, grasses and pine needles in a pine tree. 3-5 eggs.

Egg: Actual Size

Backyard Feeder

Nesting Location

Palm Warbler

Dendroica palmarum

Observation Calendar
J F M A M J J A S O N D

Male/Female: *Spring*: Rust crown that changes to brown on back of head and back; bright yellow eyebrow; brown cheeks; yellow chin and chest with rust speckles; yellow belly; rump yellow; wings and tail black and brown with white edges; feet and legs black; black bill. *Fall*: Overall browner and duller.

Did you know? The Palm Warbler is nicknamed the "wagtail warbler" and "yellow tip-up" because of its habit of bobbing its tail continuously while feeding.

Voice: Song is *zee zee zee* that rises. Call is sharp *suuup*.
Food: A variety of insects and weed seeds.
Nest/Eggs: Nest of dry grass and weed stalks, lined with fine grass, at the base of a tree or shrub. 3-5 eggs.

Bay-breasted Warbler
Dendroica castanea

Foot: Anisodactyl

Male: *Spring*: Deep rust patch on top of black head; rust on chin and along sides of chest; grey back with black banding; two white wing bars; wings and tail are black with white edges; belly white with soft rust on sides; rump white; buff patch on either side of neck; feet and legs black with hints of red. *Fall:* head changes to olive/yellow; back is yellow/olive; chest is white with pink on sides; rump is buff.
Female: Duller with less rust on neck and sides.

Did you know? The quickest way to identify the Bay-breasted Warbler is to locate the buff patch on the side of the neck.

Voice: Difficult to distinguish from other warblers. Song is high pitched *seetsy seetsy seetsy*. Call *see*.
Food: A variety of tree-dwelling insects.
Nest/Eggs: Loosely woven cup nest built of twigs, dried grass and spider's web, lined with small roots, hair and fine grasses, in tree or shrub, 4-8 metres above ground. 4-7 eggs.

Nesting Location

Blackpoll Warbler

Dendroica striata

Observation Calendar
J F M A M J J A S O N D

Male: *Spring*: Black head with white cheeks; back grey with black banding; wings and tail black with white edges; chin white; chest white with black banding; rump white; two white wing bars; feet and legs black and red. *Fall*: Olive-green overall with light banding on sides.

Female: Olive on top with thin black banding; back olive with black banding; wings and tail black with white edges, two white wing bands; chin and chest grey with small specks of black; belly grey.

Voice: High-pitched *zi zi zi zi zi* growing louder. Call is *chip*.

Food: A variety of insects.

Nest/Eggs: Bulky cup built with small twigs, grasses, weeds and moss, lined with hair, plant fibres and feathers, in conifer tree or shrub, about 2 metres above ground. 4-5 eggs.

Cerulean Warbler

Dendroica cerulea

Foot: Anisodactyl

Observation Calendar

J F M A M J J A S O N D

Male: Cerulean (sky-blue) upperparts; black streaks along white chest; black breast band; white wing bars; grey feet and legs.
Female: Turquoise-blue upperparts; bluish crown; light cream chest and belly with faded banding.

Egg: Actual Size

Voice: Medium-pitched quick *buzzzzz* sound ending with high note. Call is *chip*.
Food: Flying insects.
Nest/Eggs: Saucer built with grasses, tree bark and weeds high in the canopy of deciduous trees. 3-5 eggs.

Nesting Location

Black-and-white Warbler

Mniotilta varia

Observation Calendar
J F M A M J J A S O N D

Male: Black-and-white striped from crown down entire body length; feet and legs charcoal; bill is thin and black with thin yellow line at mouth opening.
Female: Similar to the male except striping on chest and belly is grey and white, throat is white.

Voice: Seven or more squeaky calls *weesee, weesee, weesee, weesee, weesee, weesee, weesee.*
Food: A variety of insects, mainly gypsy moths and tent caterpillars.
Nest/Eggs: Cup built of leaves, grass, hair and bark, at base of tree or near a boulder. 4-5 eggs.

American Redstart

Setophaga ruticilla

Foot: Anisodactyl

Observation Calendar

J F M A M J J A S O N D

Male: Black overall with large orange bands on wings and outer tail feathers; bright red/orange patch on side of chest; belly white; feet and legs black.

Female: Overall olive-grey with large yellow bands on wings and tail; white eyering, broken; yellow on sides of white chest; white belly; feet and legs black.

Voice: Song is a series of high-pitched thin notes ending downward. Call is *chip*.

Food: A variety of insects, wild berries and seeds.

Nest/Eggs: Compact woven cup built with plant down and grass, lined with weeds, hair and feathers, covered on the outside with lichens, plant down and spider's web, in woodlands and swamps. 4 eggs.

Egg: Actual Size

Backyard Feeder

Nesting Location

Prothonotary Warbler

Protonotaria citrea

Observation Calendar

J F M A M J J A S O N D

Male: Bright yellow overall; black-grey wings and tail; sharp black bill; feet and legs black; white highlights in tail and underparts.

Female: Similar but with olive highlights on crown, nape and back; grey wings.

Did you know? The Prothonotary Warbler prefers to build its nest in an abandoned woodpecker hole.

Voice: Loud *zweeet*, repeated in a series at the same pitch. Call is a loud *tinc*.

Food: Insects, spiders.

Nest/Eggs: Cavity built and lined with twigs, mosses and grasses. 4-6 eggs.

Ovenbird

Seiurus aurocapillas

Observation Calendar

J F M A M J J A S O N D

Male/Female: Olive overall with distinctive mark on head that is orange outlined in black, running from bill to the back of the neck; chest white with black speckles; bill dark on top with yellow on underside; black eyes surrounded by white.

Voice: A progressively louder, *teecher, teecher, teecher, teecher.*
Food: Snails, slugs, worms, spiders and most insects.
Nest/Eggs: Covered bowl, with side entry made of dead leaves, grass, moss and bark, lined with small roots, fibres and hair, on ground in depression. 3-5 eggs.

Northern Waterthrush

Seiurus noveboracensis

Size Identification

Foot: Anisodactyl

Egg: Actual Size

Observation Calendar

J F M A M J J A S O N D

Male/Female: Brown head and back with distinctive yellow eyebrow running to back of head; chest pale yellow with dark pronounced banding running down to lower belly; legs pink and red; bill black and pink; short tail.

Voice: A ringing song which drops off at the end. Call is a metallic *chink*.

Food: A variety of insects and water bugs, crustaceans, small fish, mollusks.

Nest/Eggs: Cup or dome of moss, twigs, bark and leaves, lined with moss, hair and fine grass, on ground in upturned roots or fallen trees. 4-5 eggs.

Nesting Location

Mourning Warbler

Oporornis philadelphia

Size Identification

Foot: Anisodactyl

Observation Calendar

J F M A M J J A S O N D

Male: Grey hood with olive back; yellow chest and belly with black collar; bill black with pale underparts; wings and tail dark with yellow edges; feet and legs brown.
Female: Hood is duller; broken white eye ring; wings and tail olive ending in black with white edges; chest pale grey.

Egg: Actual Size

Voice: Loud ringing *chirry chirry chirry chorry.*
Food: A variety of insects and spiders.
Nest/Eggs: Bulky cup of leaves, vines, grass, weeds and bark, lined with fine grasses, rootlets and hair, on or near ground. 3-5 eggs.

Nesting Location

Common Yellowthroat

Geothlypis trichas

Observation Calendar
J F M A M J J A S O N D

Male: Yellow chin, chest and belly contrast with a dark black mask, which runs from bill, around eyes to lower neck; white line blends into an olive head, back, wings and tail; feet and legs grey.
Female: Light brown without the distinctive mask.

Voice: A very high-pitched song, *witchity witchity witchity* that is heavily accented.
Food: Caterpillars, beetles, ants and other small insects.
Nest/Eggs: Bulky cup of grass, reeds, leaves and moss, lined with grass and hair, on or near ground, in weed stalks or low bushes. 3-5 eggs.

Hooded Warbler

Wilsonia citrina

Observation Calendar

J F M A M J J A S O N D

Male/Female: Distinct yellow mask set against black head; large black eye; chest and belly yellow; greenish-olive back; feet and legs black.

Voice: Two note *wee-taa* repeated. Call is *chink*.
Food: Flying insects on the wing, other insects, spiders.
Nest/Eggs: Cup-shaped nest built of dried leaves, twigs and plant fibres, in a shrub. 3-5 eggs.

Wilson's Warbler

Wilsonia pusilla

Observation Calendar

J F M A M J J A S O N D

Male: Black patch on top of olive-green head; back olive-green; face, cheeks, chin and belly yellow; wings and tail black with white and yellow edges; feet and legs red-pink; short bill, black with red along opening.

Female: Similar to male except the amount of black patch on top varies.

Voice: Song is a short series of *chet chet chet*.
Food: A variety of insects, including flying insects, and berries.
Nest/Eggs: Concealed cup nest built of grass, leaves and some hair, on ground at base of tree. 4-6 eggs.

Canada Warbler

Wilsonia canadensis

Foot: Anisodactyl

J F M A M J J A S O N D

Male: Dark greyish-blue head and back; eyes have white and yellow ring; black under eyes; yellow under chin extends to lower belly with a band of black speckles across chest similar to a necklace; wings and tail black edged in white; black bill has grey underside; white rump.

Female: Duller overall with black speckled necklace across chest being very faint.

Egg: Actual Size

Voice: Richly varied musical song starting with a chip.

Food: A variety of insects including beetles, mosquitoes and larvae of moths and flies.

Nest/Eggs: Bulky cup nest built of weeds, bark and leaves, lined with rootlets, plant down and hair, on or near ground in moss-covered area. 3-5 eggs.

Nesting Location

Yellow-breasted Chat

Icteria virens

Observation Calendar

J F M A M J J A S O N D

Male/Female: Olive-green upperparts; yellow chin and breast; white belly and rump; white eyebrow; black feet and legs.

Food: Insects, fruits, berries.
Voice: Various whistles and rattling sounds. Call is *chack*.
Nest/Eggs: Bulky cup of leaves built with shredded straw and grasses in small tree or bush. 3-5 eggs.

Scarlet Tanager

Piranga olivacea

Foot: Anisodactyl

Egg: Actual Size

Observation Calendar

J F M A M J J A S O N D

Male: Scarlet red from head to rump with dark black wings and tail; bill is dull yellow; feet and legs black.
Female: Olive-yellow overall with black-grey wings and tail.

Voice: Call is a *chip burr* while its song is a buzzing *querit queer queery querit queer* that is well spaced out.
Food: A variety of insects and fruit.
Nest/Eggs: Flat and flimsy cup nest on farthest branches in tree or shrub, sometimes far from the ground. 3-5 eggs.

Nesting Location

Eastern Towhee

Pipilo erythrophthalmus

Size Identification

Foot: Anisodactyl

Egg: Actual Size

Backyard Feeder

Birdhouse Nester

Nesting Location

Observation Calendar

J F M A M J J A S O N D

Male: Distinctive black head with black bill; rust-red sides and vent; white belly; feet and legs pinkish-grey; black back with white banding; long black tail with white oval-shaped underparts.

Female: Similar to male but with brown head, back and tail; white belly.

Voice: Whistle followed by a trill in two notes. Sounds like "*drink your tea*." Call is a quick *chewink*.

Food: Variety of insects, snakes, lizards, weeds and spiders.

Nest/Eggs: Built of twigs and leaves with softer grasses lining inside, placed in depression in ground. 2-6 eggs.

American Tree Sparrow

Spizella arborea

Observation Calendar

J F M A M J J A S O N D

Male/Female: Rust on top of head with light grey face, rust band running through eye; chin, chest and belly grey with a faint dark grey spot on chest; wings and tail brown and black with white edge; two white wing bars; short pointed bill is grey on top with yellow underside; feet and legs are red-black, rump grey.

Voice: Call is *te el wit.*
Food: A variety of weed seeds and tree seeds.
Nest/Eggs: Cup nest, low in tree or shrub. 4 eggs.

Chipping Sparrow
Spizella passerina

Size Identification

Foot: Anisodactyl

Egg: Actual Size

Backyard Feeder

Observation Calendar

J F M A M J J A S O N D

Male/Female: *Summer*: Bright rust crown with grey face that has a black band running through eye; short pointed bill is black; chin white changing to grey for chest and belly; feet and legs pink with black; white eyebrow; wings and tail black with brown and white edges; back brown banding with black. *Winter*: Rust crown becomes duller turning brown with black streaks; bill is pale yellow and black; eyebrow changes to buff; underside changes to buff.

Voice: Song is short trill.
Food: A variety of insects on the ground. Occasionally snatches flying insects.
Nest/Eggs: Cup built with grass, weed stalks and small roots, lined with hair and grass, low in tree or shrub, up to 8 metres above ground. 4 eggs.

Nesting Location

Field Sparrow

Spizella pusilla

Size Identification

Foot: Anisodactyl

Observation Calendar

J F M A M J J A S O N D

Male/Female: Overall brown with grey speckles; reddish-brown cap; distinctive white eye ring; bright pink bill; feet and legs pinkish-grey; tail dark with brown highlights; white vent and lower belly.

Egg: Actual Size

Voice: Whistles descending and gradually increasing in speed. Calls are *chip* and trills.
Food: Various insects and seeds. May visit feeders if seeds have fallen to ground.
Nest/Eggs: Cuplike, built from a variety of grasses and positioned on ground. 3-4 eggs.

Backyard Feeder

Birdhouse Nester

Nesting Location

Vesper Sparrow

Pooecetes gramineus

Observation Calendar

J F M A M J J A S O N D

Male/Female: Light grey overall with very fine streaks of black running down entire body; short pointed bill black on top with grey underside; feet and legs grey; back banded with black; wings and tail dark grey with white edges; white ring and small chestnut patch near shoulder; white tail feathers are revealed in flight.

Did you know? The Vesper Sparrow earned its name from its song that may be heard in the evening — at vespers, when evening prayers were said in the monasteries.

Voice: A whistle of two beats, with the second being higher, followed by trills.
Food: A variety of insects, weed seeds and grain.
Nest/Eggs: Depression in ground with grass, stalks and small roots, and lined with the same. 4 eggs.

Savannah Sparrow

Passerculus sandwichensis

Size Identification

Foot: Anisodactyl

Egg: Actual Size

Observation Calendar

J F M A M J J A S O N D

Male/Female: Black, brown and white central stripe on head; back brown with black banding; chin, chest and belly streaked with black and brown; wings and tail black with brown edges; tail is notched; bright yellow eyebrow; feet and legs red; short pointed bill is black and pink; white eye ring.

Voice: A faint, lisping *tsit tsit tsit tseeeee tsaaaay.*
Food: Main diet consists of weed seeds but will eat a variety of insects, spiders and snails.
Nest/Eggs: Scratched hollow in ground filled with grass, lined with finer grass, hair and small roots. 3-6 eggs.

Backyard Feeder

Birdhouse Nester

Nesting Location

Grasshopper Sparrow

Ammodramus savannarum

Observation Calendar

J F M A M J J A S O N D

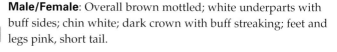

Male/Female: Overall brown mottled; white underparts with buff sides; chin white; dark crown with buff streaking; feet and legs pink, short tail.

Did you know? The Grasshopper Sparrow got its name from the buzzing sound it makes during courtship.

Voice: High pitched *buzzzzz*.
Food: Seeds, insects.
Nest/Eggs: Cup-shaped nest built with grass and rootlets, then lined with finer materials including grass and hair, in shallow depression on ground. 4-5 eggs.

Song Sparrow

Melospiza melodia

Size Identification

Foot: Anisodactyl

Egg: Actual Size

Observation Calendar

J F M A M J J A S O N D

Male/Female: Brown head and back streaked with black; buff-grey eyebrow extending to back of neck; brown band running through eye; chin, chest and belly are white with brown-black banding running down to lower belly; short pointed bill is black on top with yellow underside; red-brown crown with central white stripe; wings and tail brown with white edges; feet and legs pink; long rounded tail.

Did you know? Thoreau 'interpreted' this sparrow's song as "Maids! Maids! Maids! hang up your teakettle-ettle-ettle."

Voice: Call is a variety which includes *tsip* and *tchump*. Song is a variety of rich notes.
Food: A variety of insects, weed seeds and fruit.
Nest/Eggs: Cup close to ground with weeds, leaves and bark, lined with grass roots and hair, in tree or shrub, less than 4 metres from ground. 3-5 eggs.

Backyard Feeder

Nesting Location

Lincoln's Sparrow

Melospiza lincolnii

Observation Calendar

J F M A M J J A S O N D

Male/Female: Rust on top of head with thin grey central streak; dark grey face; buff across chest and down sides of belly with fine black streaking; belly white; feet and legs pink; wing and tail feathers black with brown edges.

Voice: Wild mixture of trills and buzzing. Calls include *tsup* and *zeee*.
Food: A variety of weed seeds and insects.
Nest/Eggs: Flat ground in bundle of grass. Built with grass, moss and lichen, lined with fine grass. 3-6 eggs.

Swamp Sparrow

Melospiza georgiana

Foot: Anisodactyl

J F M A M J J A S O N D

Male/Female: *Summer*: Top of head is reddish-brown and black; face grey with black streaks; black bill is small and sharp; chin and chest white-grey with rust along sides; back brown with black banding; wings and tail feathers brown with black ends and white edges; feet and legs pink; grey eyebrows. *Winter*: Similar to summer but both sides of chest turn darker brown and top of head is streaked with black and brown, with grey central stripe.

Egg: Actual Size

Put on your hip waders to spot this bird. It spends its summers near swamps and bogs.

Voice: Song is an unbroken musical trill. Call is *chip*.
Food: A variety of insects and seeds.
Nest/Eggs: Bulky cup built with grass, lined with finer grass, in tussock of grass or in low shrub. 3-6 eggs.

Nesting Location

White-throated Sparrow

Zonotrichia albicollis

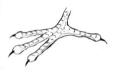

Observation Calendar
J F M A M J J A S O N D

Male/Female: Top of head is black with white central stripe; white eyebrows on either side that begin with yellow tint; black band running through eye followed by grey cheeks; small white bib under chin; grey chest; white belly with faint banding; wings and tail feathers black and brown with white edges; feet pink; back brown banded with black.

Voice: Whistle is *teeet teeet tetodi tetodi teetodi*. Calls are *tseet*.
Food: A variety of insects, grain, weed seeds and fruit.
Nest/Eggs: Cup built of grass, small roots, pine needles, twigs, bark and moss, lined with small roots, hair and grass. 3-5 eggs.

White-crowned Sparrow

Zonotrichia leucophrys

Size Identification

Foot: Anisodactyl

Male/Female: Black and white streaked head; brown and black mottled back; light grey chin, chest and belly; feet and legs yellow.

Did you know? For a week or two in May the White-crowned Sparrow is a fairly common visitor to backyards.

Voice: Whistled notes and call that includes a sharp-sounding *pink*.

Food: Seeds, insects.

Backyard Feeder

Nesting Location

233

Dark-eyed Junco

Junco hyemalis

Size Identification

Foot: Anisodactyl

Egg: Actual Size

Observation Calendar

J F M A M J J A S O N D

Male: Dark charcoal overall with white belly; short sharp bill is pale yellow with black at end; feet and legs dark grey; tail has white outer feathers that can be seen in flight.
Female: May be slightly paler than male.

Voice: Song is a trill in short phrases. Calls are *tsip, zeeet* or *keew keew*.
Food: A variety of insects, weed seeds and wild fruit.
Nest/Eggs: Large and compact built with grass, rootlets and hair, lined with hair, concealed low to or on ground. 4-5 eggs.

Backyard Feeder

Nesting Location

Snow Bunting
Plectrophenax nivalis

Observation Calendar
J F M A M J J A S O N D

Male: *Summer*: White overall with black wings and tail; tail has white edges; wings have large white patches on shoulder and flight feathers; feet and legs black; black bill, short and sharp. *In flight*: wings white.
Female and male in *winter* have brown and rust blotches.

Did you know? Accustomed to cold and heavy snowfall, the Snow Bunting will dig a hole in the snow to escape from a storm.

Voice: Song is a chorus of whistles. Call includes *buzzy tew*.
Food: A variety of insects, tree buds and seeds.
Nest/Eggs: Cup, low to ground, in tree or shrub. 3-5 eggs.

Nesting Location

Northern Cardinal

Cardinalis cardinalis

Size Identification

Foot: Anisodactyl

Egg: Actual Size

Backyard Feeder

Observation Calendar

J F M A M J J A S O N D

Male: Brilliant red overall with a stout red-orange bill, crested head; black mask beginning at base of bill resembling a small bib; feet dark red.

Female: Buff and grey with hints of bright red on crest, wings and back; stout red-orange bill with black mask beginning at base of bill (bib may appear smaller); feet are dark red.

Did you know? The cardinal gets its name from its bright red colour, which resembles that of the robes and hat of a Roman Catholic cardinal.

Voice: Song is a series of repeated whistles *wheit wheit wheit, cheer cheer cheer.* Also *chip.*

Food: Seeds, fruits, grains, various insects.

Nest/Eggs: Woven cup of twigs, vines, leaves and grass, 2-3 metres above ground, in dense shrubbery. 2-5 eggs.

Nesting Location

Rose-breasted Grosbeak

Pheucticus ludovicianus

Size Identification

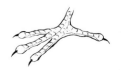
Foot: Anisodactyl

Observation Calendar
J F M A M J J A S O N D

Egg: Actual Size

Male: Large, pale yellow bill with black head; red V shape on chest; belly white with rust on either side; wings and tail black with white at edges of tail feathers visible in flight; white patches on wings; rump white; feet and legs charcoal.
Female: Buff eyebrow that extends to back of neck; brown head and back with shade of black; wings and tail brown with white edges; two white wing bars; chest and belly speckled brown; feet and legs charcoal.

Backyard Feeder

Did you know? The Rose-breasted Grosbeak is a fierce competitor when mating, clashing violently with other males. However, when it comes time to sit on the nest, the males have been known to sing.

Voice: Similar to a robin but rapid notes that are continuous *cheer-e-ly cheer-e-ly.* Call is *chink chink.*
Food: A variety of insects, tree buds, fruit and wild seeds.
Nest/Eggs: Woven grass cup in fork of deciduous tree or shrub, close to the ground. 3-6 eggs.

Nesting Location

Indigo Bunting

Passerina cyanea

Size Identification

Foot: Anisodactyl

Egg: Actual Size

Observation Calendar
J F M A M J J A S O N D

Male: Medium to deep turquoise blue overall; wide, sharp, grey beak; feet and legs black; wings and tail dark with blue highlights.
Female: Soft brown overall; buff sides and belly; faint wing bands; short conical grey beak.

Voice: Rapid series of whistles that are short and paired together — *tse tsee tew tew*. Call is short *spiit*.
Food: Insects, seeds, grain, berries.
Nest/Eggs: Compact woven cup built from stems, grasses and leaves, lined with down, in thick vegetation. 2-6 eggs.

Nesting Location

Bobolink

Dolichonyx oryzivorus

Size Identification

Foot: Anisodactyl

Observation Calendar

J F M A M J J A S O N D

Egg: Actual Size

Male: *Summer*: Black overall with pale yellow patch on back of head; back black changing to large white patch down to rump; wings have white patches and edges; feet, legs, and bill black. *In flight*: White rump is revealed; tail has sharp pointed feathers.
Female and male *(winter)*: brown and buff overall with black streaks over top of head; legs red.

Did you know? These birds need hayfield habitat to survive. Studies show that most young will die when farmers' fields are mown before they have a chance to fledge.

Voice: Song is a light phrase that increases in pitch and has been described as *bob o link - bob o link spink spank spink*. Usually sings in flight. Call is metallic *clink*.
Food: A variety of insects and weed seeds
Nest/Eggs: Slight hollow in ground with bulky gathering of grass and weed stalks, lined with fine grass, in areas near water and within waterside plants. 4-7 eggs.

Nesting Location

Red-winged Blackbird

Agelaius phoeniceus

Observation Calendar
J F M A M J J A S O N D

Male: Black overall with distinctive red shoulder patch bordered with light yellow at bottom.
Female: Brown with buff eyebrows and chin; chest and belly buff streaked with dark brown; wings and tail feathers brown with buff edges.

Did you know? Red-winged Blackbirds are prolific breeders, sometimes breeding three times in one season.

Voice: Song is *ocaaleee ocaalee*.
Food: A variety of insects and weed seeds.
Nest/Eggs: Bulky cup built of leaves, rushes, grass, rootlets, moss and milkweed fibre, lined with grass, in tall waterside plants near water. 3-4 eggs.

Eastern Meadowlark

Sturnella magna

Foot: Anisodactyl

Egg: Actual Size

Observation Calendar

J F M A M J J A S O N D

Male/Female: Bright yellow chin and throat separated by a V-shaped black collar; black on top of head with white cheeks; yellow and black band runs through eye; sides white with black speckles; back and wings black and brown with white edges; feet and legs grey; black bill is long and thin with grey underside.

Voice: Song is *teee yuuu teee yaar* repeated two to eight times.
Food: A variety of insects including grubs, beetles, grasshoppers and caterpillars. Also eats seeds and grain.
Nest/Eggs: Bulky cup in hollow on the ground in pastures, fields and marshes. Dome-shaped with a roof of interwoven grasses. 3-5 eggs.

Backyard Feeder

Birdhouse Nester

Nesting Location

Rusty Blackbird
Euphagus carolinus

Size Identification

Foot: Anisodactyl

Observation Calendar
J F M A M J J A S O N D

Male: Dull black overall with hints of green on head and bluish on wings; pale yellow eye; pointed black bill; short tail rounded at end; feet and legs black. *Winter*: Similar to summer but feathers edged in brown along with brown hints on head and wings.

Female: Overall light brown/grey with darker wings; slate-grey underparts; buff eyebrow; feet and legs black.

Did you know? The Rusty Blackbird will form large flocks in winter along with starlings and other blackbirds.

Voice: Song is extremely squeaky *koo-a-lee-meek koo-a-lee eek*, with call that is *chuk* or *kick*.

Food: Insects, salamanders, snails, small fish, grains, seeds, crustaceans.

Nest/Eggs: Small cup built from grasses and moss with a mud lining mixed with fine grass materials. Builds 2-10 feet above ground in bush or small tree usually above water. 4-5 eggs.

Nesting Location

Common Grackle

Quiscalus quiscula

Size Identification

Foot: Anisodactyl

Male: Overall iridescent black and purple; bright yellow eye; black bill long and sharp; feet and legs are charcoal grey; long tail.
Female: Similar but duller iridescent colouring, tail is shorter.

Did you know? Flocks in the thousands gather on fields and cause a lot of damage to farmers' crops.

Voice: Chatter is a metallic and rasping *grideleeeeek*. Calls are *chak chah*.
Food: A variety of ground insects, seeds, grain, minnows, rodents and crayfish.
Nest/Eggs: Loose bulky cup built with weed stalks, twigs, grass, debris, lined with feather and grass, in conifer tree or shrubs. Will occasionally use an osprey's nest. Prefers to nest in colonies. 3-6 eggs.

Egg: Actual Size

Backyard Feeder

Nesting Location

Brown-headed Cowbird

Molothrus ater

Size Identification

Foot: Anisodactyl

Egg: Actual Size

Observation Calendar
J F M A M J J A S O N D

Male: Brown head, glossy black overall; feet and legs black; sharp black bill.
Female: Overall grey with dark brown wings and tail; faint buff streaking on chest down to lower belly; feet and legs are black.

Did you know? Molothrus ater, the Cowbird's scientific name, means dark, greedy beggar, an apt name for a bird that leaves its eggs for other birds to hatch.

Voice: A squeaky *weee titi*.
Food: A variety of insects, weed seeds, grain and grass.
Nest/Eggs: Parasite. Builds no nest. 1 egg.

Nesting Location

244

Baltimore Oriole

Icterus galbula

Foot: Anisodactyl

J F M A M J J A S O N D

Male: Black head; bright orange body; black wings with orange spur and white banding; tail is black with orange along edges; legs and feet grey; long sharp grey beak.
Female: Browner than male with olive-yellow on rump; orange-yellow chest and belly; head and back mix of black, orange and brown; throat blotched; tail brown-orange.

Egg: Actual Size

Did you know? Baltimore Orioles can be attracted to feeders with orange slices or sugar solutions.

Backyard Feeder

Voice: Song is a note whistled four to eight times. Call is a two-note *teetoo* and rapid chatter *ch ch ch ch.*
Food: Insects, flower nectar, fruit.
Nest/Eggs: Plant fibre that hangs from branches. 4-6 eggs.

Nesting Location

Purple Finch
Carpodacus purpureus

Observation Calendar
J F M A M J J A S O N D

Male: Red upper parts with black banding on back; rump is red; chest is red with white feathers banding down to lower belly, which is all white; wings and tail are black with white edges; bill is broad and yellow; feet and legs grey.
Female: Brown with white eyebrow and brown eyeline; chest white with brown streaks down front; wings and tail dull brown with white edges; feet and legs grey.

Voice: Song is long and musical ending in downward trill. Call *chirp*.
Food: A variety of insects, berries, weed seeds, and buds of trees.
Nest/Eggs: Shallow cup built with twigs, grass, bark strips and small roots, lined with grass and hair, in evergreen tree or shrub, 5-60 feet above ground. 3-5 eggs.

House Finch

Carpodacus mexicanus

Size Identification

Foot: Anisodactyl

Observation Calendar

J F M A M J J A S O N D

Male: Red crown, chin and chest, which changes to buff at belly; wings and tail brown; feet and legs grey; grey bill; white undertail; dark brown banding around the sides.
Female: All greyish brown with faint banding down sides.

Voice: Musical warble ending with *jeeeer*.
Food: Weed seeds, fruit, buds.
Nest/Eggs: Cup of lined weed and grass, roots, feathers, string and twigs, 1-2 metres above ground. 4-5 eggs.

Egg: Actual Size

Backyard Feeder

Nesting Location

White-winged Crossbill

Loxia leucoptera

Observation Calendar

J F M A M J J A S O N D

Male: Overall pinkish-red with long black bill that crosses over at the end; wings and tail black, with two large white bars; lower belly turns grey; feet and legs charcoal.
Female: Similar to male except greyish with olive areas on back and head, yellow on chest and rump.

Did you know? Their bills are used to extract conifer seeds by forcing open the cone and pulling seeds out. It is an occasional breeder in the area and seen erratically.

Appear in large numbers in wooded areas near the shore.

Voice: Call to each other *peeet* with a flight call of *chif chif*.
Food: Conifer seeds, variety of insects, other seeds.
Nest/Eggs: Deep cup built with twigs, small roots, weed stalks, moss, lichen, and bark, lined with grass, feather and hair, in spruce tree or shrub, 2-3 metres above ground. 2-5 eggs.

Common Redpoll

Carduelis flammea

Observation Calendar

J F M A M J J A S O N D

Male: Red to orange cap; brown streaking on white overall; black/brown wings with two narrow wing bars; black chin; bright rose breast and sides; brown banding on sides.
Female: Red to orange cap; brown on back of head; breast is light with brown banding down sides.

Voice: Series of trills includes *chit* during flight, *chit-chit-chit-chit*. Call is *sweeeeet*.
Food: A variety of grass, tree and weed seeds, as well as insects in summer.
Nest/Eggs: Cup shape built of small twigs and lined with softer materials including moss, plant material and animal fur. Built in dense brush low to the ground. 4-7 eggs.

Pine Siskin

Carduelis pinus

Observation Calendar
J F M A M J J A S O N D

Male/Female: Brown with buff chest and belly banded with brown; long pointed bill is grey; wings and tail dark with yellow edges; feet and legs grey.

Did you know? Two points of identification of the Pine Siskin are its size and the song, which it sings in flight.

Voice: Light rasping *tit i tit* and louder *cleeeip.* Similar to a Goldfinch but deeper and coarser.
Food: Conifer seeds, weed seeds, nectar, flower buds and a variety of insects.
Nest/Eggs: Large shallow cup built with twigs, grass, moss, lichen, bark and small roots, lined with moss, hair and feathers in a conifer tree well out from trunk, 6 metres above ground. 2-6 eggs.

American Goldfinch

Carduelis tristis

Foot: Anisodactyl

Observation Calendar

J F M A M J J A S O N D

Male: *Summer*: Bright yellow overall with black forehead and yellow bill; black wings with white bands; tail black with white edges; rump white; feet and legs red. *Winter*: Yellow is replaced by grey with hints of yellow.

Female and male *(winter)*: Similar except overall grey/brown with yellow highlights.

Voice: Sing as they fly with a succession of chips and twitters, *per chic o ree per chic o ree.*

Food: A variety of insects but mostly interested in thistle and weed seeds.

Nest/Eggs: Neat cup built with fibres woven together, lined with thistle and feather down, in leafy tree or shrub in upright branches, 1-5 metres above ground. 4-6 eggs.

Egg: Actual Size

Backyard Feeder

Nesting Location

Evening Grosbeak

Coccothraustes vespertinus

Size Identification

Foot: Anisodactyl

Observation Calendar

J F M A M J J A S O N D

Male: Dark brown/black head with dull yellow stripe across forehead that blends into a dull yellow at the shoulders; tail and wings are black with hints of white; chest and stomach dull yellow; stout pale yellow bill and dark pink feet.
Female: Silver grey with light hints of dull yellow on neck and sides; tail and wings are black with white edges.

Backyard Feeder

Did you know? The Evening Grosbeak was mostly seen in western Canada until recent times when it moved east and north and can now be found in many parts of the Maritimes.

Voice: Call is a ringing *cleer* or *clee-ip*. When there is a flock of birds calling they sound like sleighbells.
Food: Seeds, insects various fruits and flower buds.
Nest/Eggs: Loosely woven cup of twigs and moss, lined with small roots. Conifer tree or shrub, in colonies. 3-4 eggs.

Nesting Location

House Sparrow

Passer domesticus

Size Identification

Foot: Anisodactyl

Observation Calendar

J F M A M J J A S O N D

Male: Rich brown on head with white cheeks; wings and tail striped with black; two distinct white wing bands; rump grey; throat and chest black which turns grey at belly; bill black; feet and legs pink.

Female: Dull brown with buff chin, chest and belly; light buff coloured eyebrows and yellow/grey bill.

Egg: Actual Size

Did you know? In the mid-1800s, eight pairs of House Sparrows were brought to North America from Europe to help control cankerworms in crops. The first attempt failed, but this sparrow has now become one of the most common birds in cities and towns.

Backyard Feeder

Voice: Repeated *chureep, chirup.*
Food: Insects, seed, grain, food waste.
Nest/Eggs: Takes over nests from other birds. Usually a large untidy ball of grass, weeds, some hair and feathers. 3-7 eggs.

Birdhouse Nester

Nesting Location

Index